Still, I Will Praise

The Power of Praising God
...Even When You Don't Feel Like It

Still, I Will Praise

The Power of Praising God
...Even When You Don't Feel Like It

Renée Bondi
with Nancy Curtis

PUBLICATIONS

Fort Washington, PA 19034

Still, I Will Praise
Published by CLC Publications

U.S.A.
P.O. Box 1449, Fort Washington, PA 19034

GREAT BRITAIN
51 The Dean, Alresford, Hants. SO24 9BJ

Unless otherwise noted, Scripture quotations are from the Holy Bible, New International Version, copyright © 1973, 1978, 1984 by International Bible Society. Used by permission of Zondervan Bible Publishers.

Scripture quotations marked NASB are from the New American Standard Bible®, copyright © 1960, 1962, 1963, 1968, 1971, 1972, 1973, 1975, 1977, 1995 by The Lockman Foundation. Used by permission.

Printed in the United States of America

ISBN-13 (hardcover): 978-1-61958-013-8
ISBN-13 (e-book): 978-1-61958-018-3

Dedication

To Mom, whose spiritual discipline
inspires me to this day.

Contents

Special Thanks to 9

Let's Get Started 11

1. *Choosing to Praise God* **in Times of Frustration** 17

2. *Choosing to Praise God* **in Times of Unanswered Prayer** 25

3. *Choosing to Praise God* **When You Need a Second Chance** 39

4. *Choosing to Praise God* **in Times of Waiting** 61

5. *Choosing to Praise God* **When Things Go from Bad to Worse** 75

6. *Choosing to Praise God* **in Times of Loneliness** 95

7. *Choosing to Praise God* **in Times of Great Loss** 107

8. *Choosing to Praise God* **When You Are Afraid** 117

9. *Choosing to Praise God* **When Things Look Hopeless** 129

10. *Choosing to Praise God* **from the Mountaintop** 139

Let's Talk it Over 153

Call to Action: Study Guide for Deeper Reflection 161

Special Thanks to . . .

Nancy Curtis, for your ability to craft my thoughts and capture my voice. You have been very gracious through every step of this lengthy process, and I am truly grateful for all you have brought to this project. I could never have done it without you.

David Almack and all the kind people at CLC Publications, for accepting my idea of pairing contemporary stories with biblical in the hopes of reminding the reader of the relevancy of God's Holy Word today.

Laura Pollard, for your gentle spirit, caring heart and most importantly, for adjusting your plans in order to see this project to completion.

Kathleen Eaton, Jana Alayra, Stewart Fischer and Nanette Osborn, for the joy each one of you have brought to my heart—not only by your sweet friendship, but also by allowing your stories to be shining spotlights on God's unending faithfulness.

Mike Bondi, for the many evenings you came home after work to see me crooked in my wheelchair from too many hours at the computer and would quickly make the much needed adjustment without one ounce of complaint. What an incredible gift you are to me! I love you so much.

Daniel Bondi, for the many after-school moments when you were wise to ask, "Is there anything else you need, Mom?" before taking your time to relax. You are so insightful and kindhearted. Thank you for your help, and I love you very much.

Deborah Winders, for your years of patience, love and understanding. You continue to be an anchor to Bondi Ministries and to me personally.

Debbi Robertson and Jan Terranova, for truly giving care to me (and my family!) on a regular basis. Thank you for your prayer, hard work, and for loving me through my tough mornings.

Let's Get Started

MUCH has been written and many sermons have been preached about praising God, but how many of us really devote ourselves to lavishing praise and adoration on our Savior? Sure, we praise God when we get a new job, we shout "Praise the Lord!" when we win a victory over something that's been troubling us, and maybe we even dare to raise our hands during worship at church, but how many of us consider praising God when we get turned down for that job, when we feel abandoned and forgotten, and when we suffer defeat?

I now have a deep understanding about praising our Lord. Ironically, I didn't learn it from standing high on a mountaintop but from sitting in my wheelchair in the valley. Praising God on a daily basis wasn't something that came naturally to me but a discipline that had to be learned and practiced.

I cannot raise my hands high in praise, but I can raise my voice and my heart. I now know firsthand that we need to praise when the road is rocky as well as straight, when experiencing showers of blessing or storms of confusion, in periods of health and of sickness. Our situation does not alter our need to praise God; as a matter of fact, I've come to realize that one of the most important times to praise God is when we struggle. But I could never have told you that twenty-five years ago when I broke my neck.

For those of you who are not familiar with how I landed in this wheelchair, let me quickly explain. It was the middle of May 1988, and at dinner my fiancé Mike gave me my engagement ring before we were off to chaperone the high school prom at San Clemente High School where I was the choral music director. The next day I had a full day directing the music for our annual spring musical, and that night I went to bed as usual, admiring my engagement ring one last time before I turned out the light. I drifted off to sleep, and the next thing I knew I was in midair, diving off the foot of my bed. I landed on the top of my head, finishing the flip with my feet in the closet and my head against the dust ruffle. Stunned and in excruciating pain, I wondered, *What in the world just happened?* Hours later in the hospital, the doctors gave my family and me the devastating diagnosis; I had broken my neck between the fourth and fifth vertebrae and was paralyzed from my upper chest down. I was quadriplegic and would spend the rest of my life in a wheelchair. To this day, we don't have a good grasp on what happened that night. I don't have any history of sleepwalking or any kind of disease that would cause a seizure. The only thing we can think of is that I had a dream, possibly where I was diving into a pool, but I don't remember any such dream. I'm looking forward to getting the answer when I get to heaven!

During the last two decades, I've learned many life lessons. I've been in the valley of darkness and I've been on the mountaintop. One of the most valuable lessons I've learned is how important, even foundational, it is for believers to praise our Lord at all times.

But what if something goes wrong? Radically wrong! What if I get a scary diagnosis from the doctor or lose my job or have a damaging argument with a loved one—surely I don't thank and praise God then! Well, yes, I should. In First Thessalonians 5:18, Paul says, "Give thanks in all circumstances, for this is God's will for you in Christ Jesus." Notice the verse doesn't say *for* all circumstances but *in* all circumstances. You might not thank God that your boss is difficult to please, but you can thank Him that you have a job and an income. You wouldn't thank God that you had a car accident, but you could thank Him that no one was seriously injured. You probably wouldn't thank God that your washing machine broke and spilled water all over the floor, but you could thank Him that you owned a washing machine when many in third-world countries don't have that luxury. Even in challenging circumstances, you can find some reason to thank God if you look for it.

I'm sure you will agree that in difficult seasons we don't feel like praising God. We'd rather wallow in our misery. We feel more comfortable griping, complaining, fault-finding and being crabby and irritable. Let's face it: in unpleasant situations, praising God is not our natural instinct. That's what the writer of Hebrews calls a "sacrifice of praise" (13:15). A sacrifice of praise means that we offer honor and praise to God whether our circumstances are good or bad, whether we feel like it or not. It's a discipline.

So if it's unnatural, if it's a discipline, then why do it? Because our praise brings us to the heart of God. Psalm 22:3 says that God inhabits the praises of His people; in other words, when we praise, God shows up! Praise and worship put God where He belongs (on the throne) and us where we belong (in submission). I've come to understand that when we take our focus off our own concerns and annoyances and place it on what a great God we serve, the weight of our problems lightens and our faith begins to soar.

Simply put, when I praise God and thank Him, it reminds me that God is God, and I am not. It puts the world back into perspective and I get my spiritual equilibrium back.

Remember, though, that praising God and thanking God are closely related, but different. Praise is worshipping and honoring God for who He is—the Creator, the Lamb of God who takes away the sins of the world, the Good Shepherd, the Everlasting Father,

Messiah, the Prince of Peace, the great I Am. Acknowledging His greatness—that's praise. But then we *thank* God for what He has done for us. We thank Him for our family, health, job, home and friends, for that unexpected phone call that brightened our day, for the beautiful sunset, for timing that kept us from being in an accident, for the fun day we had at the park, etc. So praising and thanking God are different but are equally important. I confess that I've been rather loose with the terms in this book and have used them interchangeably, but the central point to remember is that God deserves to be worshiped both for who He is and for what He has done!

So this is what this book is about—praising God when we feel like it and praising God when we don't. It may or may not change your circumstances, but I promise that it will change your focus, which will change your mind and then your heart and, as a result, your entire attitude.

I pray that in these pages you'll find inspiration to love the Lord more fully and to praise and thank Him more often. May God touch your heart and bless you with His presence as you read *Still, I Will Praise*.

> *I have suffered very much;*
> *preserve my life, O LORD, according to your word.*
> *Accept, O LORD, the willing praise of my mouth,*
> *and teach me your laws.*
> *Psalm 119:107–8*

1

Choosing to Praise God
IN TIMES OF FRUSTRATION

PURE frustration was the catalyst that started my journey toward learning to praise God in all situations. I was facing having to train not one but two new attendants. Being in a wheelchair and not having the use of my arms or legs, I am dependent on caregivers for the daily routine of things other people can do for and by themselves, like going to the bathroom, bathing, brushing my teeth, blow-drying my hair and dressing, to name just a few. I have an attendant in my home three hours every morning just to help me get ready for the day. Unfortunately, even if caregivers are experienced in assisting others, they still have to be trained to my particular needs. They need to know where things are stored in our home, how to adjust me comfortably in my wheelchair and how to keep my hair from looking frizzy.

Let's face it. Even though they're wonderful people, I really don't want to have attendants in the first place. I want to be able to take my own bath by myself, style my own hair, drive my own van and blow my own nose just like any other woman, so I have to deliberately use self-control in not taking my resentment out on those who are there to help me! On good days there's no problem. On bad days I have to watch myself. Trust me—it's not a good thing when the person you've just snapped at is brushing your hair!

Having to train new caregivers is always a strain, but this one time I was particularly overwhelmed. I had just completed a very taxing year (the one year I'd returned to teaching) when the economy took a downturn and two of my caregivers had to resign to pursue full-time positions. As a teacher, I had to explain and exercise patience with my students, but by the time school was out, I was tired of explaining and had exhausted my supply of patience. Just when I needed to be free of those disciplines, I was looking at weeks of practicing both. It was almost more than I could handle. My patience and tactfulness were at an all-time low. I didn't think I could nicely explain one more time how to put my pants on or how to get my hand in the wrist brace I use to eat and type. But like it or not, I had to push through and do it. It was not optional. I had to have new caregivers, and no one could train them for me.

About that time I began observing how other Christians I knew seemed to be so joyful when I knew they were carrying heavy loads. They seemed to have a peace and a joy that superseded their problems. I wondered how they could smile so warmly, be interested in others and have a positive attitude when their hearts were broken. They managed to praise God no matter what! I knew I wasn't there, and I wanted to be.

So I went to my Bible concordance and looked up every time the word "praise" was used. There were a gazillion entries. Being the person I am, I wanted to read them all. Hours and hours later, I figured out that I simply couldn't read every verse in one sitting. I decided to narrow my field a bit, so I looked up the times "praise" was used when people in the Bible were facing daunting tasks. I wanted to see how biblical characters praised the Lord when they were confronted with mountains.

I found myself totally enamored with the story of King David and his preparation for the building of the temple in First Chronicles 22 and 23. David wanted to be the one to build the temple to honor God and house the Ark of the Covenant. However, God told David that he had shed too much blood and had made too many wars, so God passed the responsibility (and the honor) of building the temple to David's son Solomon and ensured a time of peace during his reign so this great task could be accomplished.

When we pick up the story, David is preparing to abdicate the throne to pass the kingship on to his son Solomon. David wants to make sure that the temple is "exceedingly magnificent, famous and glorious." Because Solomon is too young and inexperienced for such an undertaking, David is arranging for the building of the temple before his death. He tells Solomon that he has prepared one hundred thousand talents of gold and one million talents of silver along with bronze and iron beyond measure. He had prepared timber and stone and workmen in abundance—woodsmen and stonecutters and all types of skillful men for every task.

Now here's the part that caught my attention. When David passed the kingship onto Solomon, he gathered together all the leaders of Israel. Now follow these numbers closely. There were thirty-eight thousand Levites, and David divided them into four areas of responsibility: twenty-four thousand were to look after the work of the house of the Lord, six thousand were officers and judges, four thousand were gatekeepers and four thousand were to praise God with the musical instruments that King David himself had made. Did you catch that? David assembled *four thousand* men to do nothing but praise the Lord. And he even made musical instruments for that very purpose. I'm trying to picture even one person walking around a construction site these days with the assignment to do nothing but praise the Lord!

Fascinated, I kept reading. In Second Chronicles 5 I picked up the end of the story concerning the dedication of the completed temple. What a spectacle it must have been! When they brought in the Ark of the Covenant—the symbol of God's presence with them, which

held the original tables on which the Ten Commandments were inscribed—to place it in the Holy of Holies,
the Levites stood at the east end of the altar dressed
in white linen. They had cymbals, stringed instruments
and harps, and with them were one hundred and twenty men with trumpets. Together the singers lifted their
voices as the instruments rang out, and they praised the
Lord singing,

> He is good;
> his love endures forever. (5:13)

Now that was a symphony of praise! And at that
moment the temple was filled with a cloud of the glory
of God so big that the priests could not continue ministering because of it!

Picture this in your mind! All those men robed in
white, all kinds of musical instruments and a heavenly choir all there for one purpose—to praise God! My
guess is that their worship was so loud it could be heard
all the way to the Mediterranean Sea. Awesome!

Then Solomon spoke to the people and recounted
how his father David had had it in his heart to build the
temple but how God assigned it to the next generation.
Then Solomon, the king of Israel, bowed down before
the huge assembly, lifted his hands toward heaven and
prayed, "O LORD, God of Israel, there is no God like
you in heaven or on earth—you who keep your covenant of love with your servants who continue wholeheartedly in your way" (6:14).

Think about it. Solomon was king, and kings don't bow—not to anybody! People bow to the king, not the other way around. It's a pride thing; it's a statement of position, authority and superiority. But Solomon kneeled in front of the entire country, demonstrating his submission, love and devotion to the almighty God who is the ultimate king and authority.

Solomon went on to praise God by marveling that He actually could and would live on earth and dwell in the temple made with hands. God choosing to dwell among sinful people in this way foreshadowed the time when He would walk the earth in the form of Jesus Christ—our Messiah who lived among sinful people and died to redeem us and carry us back to heaven. What an amazing God we serve!

By the time I finished reading about David, Solomon and the temple, I was convicted. It was obvious to me that praise had a huge role in the building of the temple and in God's response of dwelling there. *Well,* I thought to myself, *if King David, a man after God's own heart, and his son Solomon, the wisest man who ever lived, thought it was that important to praise God during the building and dedication of the temple, then evidently praise is something I need to be practicing more in my life.*

But then there was that caregiver thing I was facing. One night I lay in bed and prayed, *Lord, I've always wanted to be a person who praises You even when things are painful. I'm sorry I have not done this in the past, but*

I want to begin today. So out of obedience, I'm going to start praising You every time these new gals walk through the door.

And so it began. When one of my new attendants appeared, I prayed inside, *I praise You, Lord. I lift Your name on high. You are amazing. You are powerful. You are holy. You are everything, and I praise You! I praise You!* And I continued praising the Lord as I instructed my new caregivers. When they were bathing me, I glorified the Lord. When I was telling them how to comb my hair, I was praising God. When I instructed them on how to lock down my chair in the latches in the van, I worshiped Jesus. When I wanted to snap at them for doing something wrong or for not knowing how to perform a task, I glorified God instead. I didn't feel like it; it was my sacrifice of praise.

One day I was sharing my struggle with my friend Joni Eareckson Tada (speaker, singer, author and the founder of Joni and Friends International Disability Center). Being quadriplegic for over forty years, she understood my struggle of training new caregivers, and she told me one of her strategies. When the caregiver comes through the door, she says, *Lord, I don't have a smile for this woman who's coming in right now. But You do. I add to that—so please smile through me.*

After a few weeks of my intentional praising, my husband Mike commented, "Boy, Renée, you sure sailed through training your attendants this time! I didn't hear you complain at all!"

"Really? You've got to be kidding me!" It hadn't occurred to me until he said it, but he was right. Training my caregivers was not the odious task that I had imagined it would be. The reason was obvious: I praised God and thanked Him instead of wallowing in self-pity and resentment.

And so began my journey of learning how to praise. I learned right away that it was a choice to praise or to be impatient, to worship or to wage war, to let God respond in me or to respond in my own frustration. I was beginning to learn that honoring and worshiping God, even in the dark times, is key to living the abundant life Jesus promised.

2

Choosing to Praise God

IN TIMES OF UNANSWERED PRAYER

WHEN we pray for something, we typically ask God to do exactly what we want, the way we want, when we want it done. If He doesn't, we may feel He didn't answer our prayer, and we may become irritated and even disillusioned. We may start doubting that God listens or responds.

Wouldn't it be great if there were some formula that could guarantee the desired response to our prayers? Something like, if I prayed for something twenty-five times and gave one hundred dollars to the church, then I'd get the results I want. But we all know it doesn't work that way. We pray for someone to be healed; sometimes he recovers, and sometimes his healing is when he enters heaven. We pray for a job; sometimes we're hired the next day, and sometimes we wait for months. We pray for a teenager to seek help for his drug addiction; sometimes we see a move in the right direction, and sometimes we watch as his habit escalates. In short, we pray in faith. Sometimes we get the answer we want, and sometimes we don't.

The New Testament is full of instances of Jesus or His disciples healing the sick, the blind, the lame, the leper. There are even a few times when the dead were raised! Everyone Jesus touched was healed—without exception.

One of my favorite examples of someone being healed is found in John 5:1–9. It's pretty obvious why I would pick the story of the paralytic; we're both disabled. People who were ill came to the Pool of Bethesda because they were convinced that when the waters were "troubled," the first one who touched the water would be healed.

Now this one man had been crippled for thirty-eight years, and he had come—probably more accurately had been brought—to the pool in the hopes of being healed. However, time and time again he had been beaten out by other hopefuls who had been able to get into the water more quickly or who had had someone assist them into the pool. So the crippled man had never been first. It was doubtful he would ever make it.

In comes Jesus. He saw the crippled man and asked him what, on the surface, seems to be the silliest question in the Bible: "Do you want to be made well?" (5:6) Wouldn't anyone who was crippled or sick want to be well? Certainly most would, but there were advantages to being disabled. There were a lot of things that the disabled man would not have been able, and therefore not required, to do like go to work, feed the camels, and plant and harvest crops. So maybe Jesus was asking, "Are you willing to accept the responsibility of being able-bodied?" The paralytic replied that he could not get into the waters when they were troubled because others were faster than he. It was an indirect answer, but the implication was that he was trying his best to be whole.

Jesus didn't tell him to try harder or to bring a friend. Our Lord simply told him to get up, take up his mat and walk. And the paralytic did just that. It was that simple and that quick. The paralytic didn't even have to ask. He was completely healed.

In the summer of 2000, I visited that ancient pool in Jerusalem. Mike and I were in Jerusalem at the invitation of Kingdom Productions, a ministry organization based in Ontario, California. Martha Reyes was the producer, and she had put together a pilgrimage for people from South America to come to Israel for the two thousand year anniversary of the birth of Jesus. I was very excited to be asked to be part of this pilgrimage of eight hundred visitors.

Mike and I had wondered how difficult it would be for me to travel to Israel in a wheelchair. Praise God that the world has gotten much more accessible for the disabled when it comes to traveling, but Israel was a world away from us. We had questions like, "Will the hotel rooms be accessible? Will the doors be wide enough?

Will the shower have a lip on it so I can't roll in to take a shower? How will I charge my wheelchair with the electrical current being different?" We had many concerns, but nothing could have deterred us from going. We were so excited that we were willing to check out every detail to make sure that everything would run smoothly. After all, we were going to be there to celebrate Jesus' 2000th birthday!

We pilgrims traveled on buses from site to site. Our tour guide showed us where different events in Scripture had taken place. All the Bible stories came to life! I will never read Scripture the same way again now that I've seen where it happened. There's nothing like being on the shore of the Sea of Galilee and imagining Jesus walking on the water or calming the tempest. I'll never forget being on that slope where Jesus gave His Sermon on the Mount. Although it's been built up and commercialized a bit, I remember having a little quiet time. I felt the warm breeze on my face and heard the water gently lapping up on the shore. I leaned over and looked at the weeds and the dirt and thought, *The breeze doesn't change, and the sound of water doesn't change, and even the dirt could be the same. This could very well be what it felt like to those people sitting here on this hillside, listening to Jesus say "Blessed are the poor in spirit, for theirs is the kingdom of heaven."* I took some quiet time to pray to our Lord and visualized how it must have felt to sit there and hear Jesus give such profound truths and instruction.

We visited many of the holy sites in Israel, but I was most nervous and excited to see the Pool of Bethesda. It was not on the tour itinerary, but Mike and I were determined, for obvious reasons, to get there. I had read the story in John many times, and often, especially in the early years after my injury, I would reflect on that Scripture of Jesus healing the paralytic and think, *That's me. I know that's me.* I never said this out loud to anyone except Mike, but the fact that Jesus healed the paralytic gave me hope that He would someday heal me of my paralysis. If He did it then, He could certainly do it now.

There have been a few times in these last twenty plus years of being in a wheelchair that I have encouraged God to be the author of the story of my healing. How perfect it would be if all of a sudden I was healed! The glory would never be to me; it would only be to our huge, powerful and amazing God.

I remember thinking and praying the night before my wedding, *God, tomorrow when I come to the doors of the Basilica in San Juan Capistrano for our wedding, how perfect it would be to all of a sudden be healed, stand up from my wheelchair and walk down that long beautiful aisle! I can't imagine the glory that that would give to You! We all would be screaming and yelling Your name, Your powerful name, because You are the God of miracles!* But evidently that was my idea, not His.

Back to Jerusalem. One day when the tour was going somewhere else, Mike and I decided to make our way to the Pool of Bethesda. We enlisted the help of our wonderful Christian tour guide Emile (interestingly enough, Christian guides are rare in Israel) who told us we should go at noontime. The pool is closed to tourists then, but he knew somebody who would let us in. That morning both Mike and I were lighthearted and laughing, but the closer we got to the pool, the quieter we became.

As Emile arranged, we arrived right at lunchtime so we could have some privacy. I rolled up to the edge of the ruins. From up above in the viewing area, we could see that there were once twin pools. We traced with our eyes the paths people would have walked or rolled to the water. There's no water now. We looked around, trying to find a path that would lead us down to where the water had been, but there wasn't really a way. The public was held to the viewing area above, obviously to preserve the historic site. We had to be content to stay up top and look down.

Mike stood behind me with his hands on my shoulders. As he often does, he started massaging the tension out of my shoulder muscles and neck. Soon he leaned down, wrapped his arms around me and pressed his cheek to my face. We embraced quietly for quite some time. Then I broke the silence, praying out loud,

Lord, we praise You for allowing us to come to this holy place. Thank You for putting it on Martha's heart to invite me. Thank You for the privilege of singing Your name in the Holy Land. We would never have guessed when I was

lying in ICU with a broken neck that we would have the opportunity to travel anywhere, let alone to this amazing place to experience the land where You walked. But now Lord, You know why we are here. Lord, this would be the most perfect time for You to grant the miracle of taking my paralysis completely away. God, I can think of the people who would come to You because of the clear, obvious message that You are the God of miracles, that You are real, that You are faithful and that You care deeply about the desires of our hearts.

Lord, I don't know if I have a deeper desire than to get out of this wheelchair. How I would love to be the kind of wife I want to be for Mike! How I would love to be an active mom for Daniel! To be able to dance or to walk on the beach with Mike or to throw a frisbee with Daniel or to pick up my nieces and nephews and take them to lunch. How great it would be to walk into my mom and dad's house and say, "Hey, I've got a little surprise for you!" and to watch their jaws drop, to see their burden taken away. Lord, I know that You can do this because You are the Creator who made the heavens and told the ocean where to be, the sun where to stand and the moon where to hide until evening.

Lord, if You will grant this miracle, I will sing Your praises louder than any daughter You have ever known. I can only imagine how people will say, "My Lord and my God" and come running to You.

Mike's and my eyes were closed with heads bowed. Mike continued praying, but I don't remember his exact words because I was too busy crying at the visual of me as an active, "normal" person.

When we finished praying, we opened our eyes, and Mike saw that I had huge tears running down my face. He untied the bandanna from around my neck and wiped my tears with it. We were silent, looking at each other, and we gradually came to the realization that the miracle was not going to occur. I looked at him and sighed deeply. "Well, I guess it's not supposed to happen. I wonder why." Then, while Mike held me, I cried and cried. I was as sad and disappointed for him as I was for myself.

We sat and stared out over the ruins for probably ten minutes, coming to a place of acceptance. The idea of coming to this place of healing had gotten me excited about the possibility of a real-life miracle, so we had to calm our hearts and our minds and try to understand that God was doing something bigger than healing my paralysis. I wanted to see the front of the needlepoint of my life at that moment because all I could see was the back and all the crisscrossing and knots, remembering that God is the weaver who sees the beautiful top side while we, here on earth, can see only the confusing underside.

I couldn't stay in that mental state too long because, after all, the wheelchair was what had gotten me to Israel and given me such special moments as singing "Bethlehem Morning" on a stage next to the Church of the Nativity, the site of Jesus' birth. I don't know if that would've happened if I hadn't broken my neck. Of course, I'll never know for sure, but I suspect that I still would have been a choral director at some high school. It would have been a good life, but I often wonder if my relationship with Jesus would be as deep or as rich if I had retained the use of my limbs. I'm not trying to say this to make myself or you feel better about the fact that God didn't allow me to walk again; I'm saying it because my relationship with Him is now one of complete dependence, and I doubt I would have had the need to be completely reliant on Him if my hands and my feet had continued to work. If I didn't have that deep relationship with Him, how could I pass that on to my son, my nieces and nephews and my friends and neighbors? I wouldn't be able to.

I thought about these realities as I sat quietly at the edge of the ruins of the Pool of Bethesda. I attempted to sort out what it all meant. I don't know if I'll ever know until I reach heaven, but this I know for sure: I would love nothing more than to be healed, not just for me but mostly for the ones who are dearest to me. But if God offered me a choice to be physically whole and do life on my own with only a nominal relationship with Him or to remain in the chair and keep my intimacy with Him and see His purposes for my life, I'd stay sitting right where I am. I can't even imagine, nor do I want to, my life without my reliance on Jesus.

Mike then gently said, "Okay, it's time. Let's go." *Leave? I have to leave?* It sounds strange, but I had that same feeling you have when you look at someone in the coffin; it's the last time you will ever see that person, so you really don't want to leave. You know it's just the body and the soul isn't there, but something in you doesn't want to believe it's over. I had that same feeling. I felt that if the healing didn't happen there, it never would, so I wanted to stay. I sat quietly a few more minutes just looking at the pool area, and then I inhaled big and sighed and prayed again. *Okay, God, this is the way it is and the way it is going to be. I really don't like it and I'm disappointed, but I'll keep going. Use me however You want and continue to bring meaning to this journey.* I put my hand on the joystick of my chair and turned away from the pool. Mike put his hand on my shoulder, and we headed back out onto the streets of Jerusalem.

Unanswered prayer. Even Paul knew it. He revealed in Second Corinthians 12:7 that he had a "thorn in the flesh." Many scholars speculate as to the exact nature of that "thorn"; some suggest that it might have been an oozy eye problem. Paul told us that he asked God, even pleaded with God, to take it from him, but it didn't happen.

I wonder, "Wouldn't it have been a powerful witness to have healed Paul?" Evidently it wouldn't have had as strong an impact as not healing him, according to God's economy. And perhaps the same holds true for me; evidently in God's opinion, I serve Him better from my chair than from my feet.

Paul believed that the thorn was given to prevent him from becoming arrogant. God wanted to remind Paul that His strength was made perfect in his weakness. So Paul accepted *and even embraced* his infirmity so that God would be glorified. Did Paul fully understand? I wonder. Would he have still preferred that God take it from him? I'm guessing yes. Nevertheless, Paul was so committed to serving God that he was eager to do whatever it took. He trusted God so completely that he wholeheartedly submitted to Him—even enduring his "thorn" if it meant he would be a better witness.

That's part of praise. In submitting to his thorn in the flesh, Paul was acknowledging that God knew more than he did. Whereas we see the present, God sees the big picture. Whereas we want what is comfortable and easy, God's priority is our growth in grace and truth. God is God, and we're not, and the bottom line is that He's more concerned about our holiness than He is about our happiness.

It is in such times that that "sacrifice of praise" I mentioned before kicks in. The writer of Hebrews admonished us to continually offer God our "sacrifice of praise" (13:15). Why a sacrifice? Because we don't always feel like it. We don't always understand. It's more natural to gripe and complain and question than it is to praise in the midst of disappointment and confusion. Yet we're to give praise continually. How? We can give praise continually by remembering God, including Him in our day and filtering whatever happens through

His perspective. This reminds us that God is God and that He's on the throne. And because He is, we can offer praise even when we don't like our circumstances.

I've thought about that day at the Pool of Bethesda many times over the years. I've also thought about others who pray, hoping and even believing for a miracle. When it doesn't happen, we have a choice to either say, "Okay, God. I don't like it, but I'm staying," or we can walk away and say, "Forget it! You don't exist." It is reassuring when I remember that there have been many times in my life when I have prayed for things like for direction, clarity or joy, and God has always delivered—*always*.

This one time He didn't, and, yes, it's a biggie, but it's at these times I think of the song lyric, "When you can't see His hand, trust His heart."

Before we move to the next chapter, consider the words of this profound poem:

THE WEAVER

My life is but a weaving
Between my Lord and me,
I cannot choose the colors
He worketh steadily.

Oft times He weaveth sorrow,
And I in foolish pride
Forget He sees the upper
And I, the underside.

Not till the loom is silent
And the shuttles cease to fly
Shall God unroll the canvas
And explain the reason why

The dark threads are as needful
In the Weaver's skillful hand
As the threads of gold and silver
In the pattern He has planned.

    —Author unknown

3

Choosing to Praise God

WHEN YOU NEED A SECOND CHANCE

THE very mention of a "second chance" implies that we've made a mistake, had an error in judgment, been unsuccessful, botched up, made a mess of things, blown it. Scripture is full of examples of God giving people who had failed a second chance. Peter denied knowing Jesus three times; John Mark deserted the missionary journey with Paul and Barnabas and returned home; Abraham tried to pass his wife off as his sister; the sons of Jacob sold their brother Joseph into slavery in Egypt; the woman at the well was living in sin—yet God extended grace to all of them.

One of my favorite stories of God's redemption is perhaps a little less well-known and a little less obvious; it's the story of Naomi in the short book of Ruth (one of two books in the Bible named after a woman). The story took place in the days before Israel had kings, when judges ruled and "every man did as he saw fit" (Judg. 17:6). It was a period of disobedience, violence and idolatry. Sound familiar?

Elimelech and Naomi and their two sons Mahlon and Kilion lived in Bethlehem, in Judah, in the Promised Land. But there was a famine in the land, so Elimelech moved his family to the country of Moab. Now understand that when God gave the Israelites the Promised Land, He told them, "Be careful to obey so that it may go well with you in the land and that you may increase greatly in the land flowing with milk and honey" (Deut. 6:3). *In the land!* He didn't say, "Dwell here unless there's a famine," or "If things get tough, run to Egypt or Damascus or Moab." No, God gave them the land and expected them to live there, close to Him and under His protection.

Moab was not a good country. The Moabites worshiped the god Chemosh (Num. 21:29; 1 Kings 11:7, 33) who accepted human sacrifices (2 Kings 3:26–27) and encouraged immorality (Num. 25). Jews were not to mix with the Moabites (Deut. 23:3). So why would a God-fearing Jew not only leave the place of God's protection but—even worse—move to a pagan country of idol-worshippers? Elimelech's flight was an indication of his lack of faith; it was a sign that he didn't believe God could take care of them in Bethlehem (which, ironically, means "House of Bread"). He took matters into his own hands and fled.

Elimelech only planned to stay in Moab "for a while" but became comfortable in the land and remained there. Unfortunately, his two sons grew up in Moab and, quite naturally, were influenced by its pagan culture. Had they grown up in Judah, they would have been influenced by the stories of the one true God's faithfulness to His people—how God had given them the land, how He brought His people out of Egypt, how the Red Sea and the Jordan River had parted for them, how God had given the Israelites Jericho, how God had blessed their forefathers Abraham, Isaac and Jacob. But Mahlon and Kilion didn't have access to these stories of God because their parents traded their faith for perceived prosperity.

So what happened to their great plan? First, Elimelech died. If Naomi had been concerned about who her sons would take as wives, she would have taken them back to Bethlehem right then, before they married. But she stayed, and Mahlon and Kilion married Moabite women. Naomi evidently approved—or at least she looked the other way or rationalized that it was probably not that big a deal.

The next tragedy was that Mahlon and Kilion both died. Naomi was then alone in Moab with two Moabite daughters-in-law, so she *finally* decided to return home. I wish I could report that in deciding to return to Bethlehem she was returning to her God, but the truth is that repentance wasn't her motive. She decided to return to Bethlehem because she heard that things were better there now. Naomi's decision was right, but her motive was wrong. She was still interested primarily in getting food, not in fellowship with God. You don't hear her confessing her sins to God and asking Him to forgive her. She was returning to her land but not necessarily to her Lord.

And wouldn't it be a natural, loving gesture to encourage her daughters-in-law to go back to Judah with her and come to know the one, true, living God? Wouldn't she want to take those two young women out of that pagan country, away from idol worshiping? But no, she urged them to return to their families! Perhaps she assumed her daughters-in-law had the same priority she did to marry and live comfortably financially, or perhaps she was embarrassed to take her Moabite daughters-in-law with her because they would be a symbol to her people that she had allowed her sons to marry outside the faith. We don't know what her motives were, but it is obvious that she wasn't thinking spiritually.

Now to be fair to Naomi, she evidently had some testimony about the God of the Israelites because Ruth, one of her daughters-in-law, insisted on going with her. Ruth flatly refused to turn back, proclaiming that she wanted to be a part of Naomi's culture and to accept her God. "Where you go I will go, and where you stay I will stay. Your people will be my people and your God my God" (Ruth 1:16).

Naomi had been away from home for ten years, and the women of the town were shocked when they saw her. *Can this be Naomi?* Naomi was not the woman they had known a decade before; her sorrowful years in Moab had taken their toll on her appearance and personality.

Naomi replied, "Don't call me Naomi [meaning "pleasant"] . . . Call me Mara [meaning "bitter"], for I went away full, but the Lord has brought me back empty" (1:20). Instead of making her better, life's trials had made her bitter. She accused God of dealing very harshly with her. She had left Bethlehem with a husband and two sons and had come home without them. She had gone to Moab with possessions and had returned home with nothing. She was a woman with empty hands, an empty home and an empty heart. Because she didn't surrender to the Lord and accept His loving chastening, she did not experience His presence and peace.

Sometimes we, like Naomi, bring calamity on ourselves, and sometimes life just deals us a wallop, but either way we can control how we respond to unpleasant situations. "In everything give thanks" (1 Thess. 5:18) isn't always easy to obey, but it's the best antidote for a bitter and critical spirit.

So Naomi returned to Bethlehem a broken and bitter woman. She needed a second chance, but it appears that she was so defeated and discouraged that she didn't think a renewal or happy future was possible. She thought her life was over. As it turned out, her trials were not the end but a new beginning for her! Even though Naomi had made a mess of things, God had never forgotten or stopped loving her. Quite the contrary, He had plans for her! Naomi was about to make a new beginning. With God, it's never too late to start over again. God is a God of second chances. Isn't that encouraging—that when we fail, God doesn't forget us and still has plans for us?

Naomi was bitter, but Ruth trusted God and was as committed to Him as she was to her mother-in-law. God began His gracious work with Ruth. Naomi soon learned that God's hand of blessing was on this young woman and that He would accomplish great things through her obedience. Ruth influenced Naomi, and then God brought blessings unimaginable.

I wish I had time and space to tell you all the details, but you can (and I hope you will!) read it for yourself in the short, four-chapter book of Ruth. At the end of the story, Ruth marries Boaz, a godly, generous and gentle landowner. Ruth was no longer a Moabitess but was now the wife of Boaz, a name she could be proud to bear. The old was gone; she had a new beginning. She gave birth to a son and called him Obed. Aged Naomi now had an heir.

Obed was a special child, giving new life to the family. You can imagine Naomi's joy in holding this new baby boy on her lap. When he grew up, he had a son named Jesse, and Jesse had a son named David—King David. And from the line of King David came our Lord and Savior Jesus Christ! When Naomi returned to Bethlehem bitter and broken, she could not have imagined such a happy ending!

The book of Ruth starts in Moab and ends in Bethlehem. It begins with three funerals and ends with a wedding and a birth. Naomi was hopeless, but by the end she's filled with joy. She was downhearted, but God restored her hope. Naomi's mistakes weren't fatal, and her failure wasn't final. With God, they never are.

A dear friend of mine sojourned in "Moab" and, like Naomi, she learned that God is a God of second chances. Let me introduce you to Kathleen Eaton. I want you to hear her story.

I was raised with five other siblings in a tumultuous Irish home. Dad was a drinker and a gambler. The gambling was a source of enormous pain and suffering in our family when I was growing up. Because of it, my dad got into trouble in Seattle (where I was born), and when I was thirteen, my parents lost everything and we moved to California.

We were very poor. The nine of us lived in a small, three-bedroom, one-bathroom house. It had a washer but no dryer, so we hung our clothes out to dry. If we had anything good, Dad would pawn it, so our furniture was beat-up. Some of the windows were covered in cardboard, and the carpet was ripped. Our little Catholic church would bring bags of food and put them on our porch.

I arrived at my new California school when I was in junior high, and I didn't have the right anything. We'd go to the clothing bank at church to get my clothes, and one time I found this cute little blue and beige pin-striped skirt with a beige blouse, and it fit me. Because I was tall and lanky, that didn't happen often, so I was very excited!

I felt good about how I looked when I went to choir practice at church, but the "in crowd," the perfect girls, were behind me, and I heard one of them say to the others, "Oh my gosh! She's got my clothes on." And then she started making fun of me and telling me how much better the outfit looked on her and how bad I looked. Then one of the group took gum out of her mouth and used it to stick my hair to the shirt. I was devastated! I ran out of the church and swore I'd never go back.

I got my first job when I was in junior high, babysitting after school from 4 p.m. to midnight for a woman who was a stripper. Then I'd walk around the corner to our house, go to bed and get up the next morning to go to school. At age fifteen I went to work in a retail store (having told them I was sixteen), and on Saturday mornings I worked sweeping floors and cleaning sinks at a hair salon. I was determined never to be poor and never to be an outcast again. I saved the money I earned and hid it so I could get enough to move out of the house, but sometimes my dad would search my room and find my stash and take it for gambling or drinking, and I'd have to find another hiding place and start all over. By the time I was a freshman in high school, I spent as much time as I could at a girl friend's home, only going back to my house when necessary.

When I was younger, I had wanted to be a nun, but by the time I got to college, I had denounced God, saying that I'd never go to church again. I didn't believe that any god would have allowed me to go through the terror I went through every night in my house. My unhappy childhood made me determined and strong. I identified with Scarlet O'Hara in *Gone with the Wind* when she picks the carrot up off the ground and says, "I'll never go hungry again."

This was the end of the 1960s and the start of the 70s, so I hit the ground running. I went to work for AT&T and married Tom. He was a wonderful young man who came from a loving, Italian Catholic family. We soon had our first son, Christopher. There was security in that family, something I'd never experienced, and Tom gave me a wonderful sense of safety. But I didn't realize how damaged I was.

I started advancing up the corporate ladder. I was so determined and motivated that I was unstoppable; I did everything 200 percent. I was driven to become successful, and I was. I was one of the first women to accept a non-traditional job; at the company's request, I took a position as foreman of a construction crew so that AT&T could meet their quota for women doing men's jobs. When I took the crew, it ranked 31st out of 32, and a year later we were number 1. That's how driven I was—and still am.

That little girl who was a nobody and who no one liked and whose hair was never right and who wore clothes that others had discarded was now a somebody. I was living in the third home I had bought, was driving a BMW, and was on the fast track. When you've been broken and then find yourself living a life that appears to be successful and complete, you become a person you don't recognize. I didn't think I was attractive, but men did.

During my early adult years, I tried to get my mother to show her love for me. My parents weren't the kind of people who would express love; my mother didn't know how, and my dad didn't care, so I really never knew what love was. I looked for love in all the wrong places. My husband and I were separated but back together off and on, trying to work things out. I started having affairs and got pregnant by a man I worked with.

I shut down my heart and came to the conclusion that I had to have an abortion. My marriage wasn't working, and I couldn't tell Tom it wasn't his child. I couldn't do construction being pregnant. I couldn't go tell my mom that not only was my marriage falling apart but that I was pregnant with another man's baby. I thought there was no way out. So I found a family planning clinic in the phone book and went in the next morning. They gave me a brief little spiel about how "it" was only a blob of tissue—blah blah blah. I never stopped and thought about it. I didn't really care. I was just numb.

That was 1980. I hadn't been in church in eight years. I didn't pray, and although I didn't say it, I really didn't believe in God. I hadn't been home in years. The night before the abortion, I drove over to my mom and dad's apartment, went in and asked if I could spend the night. I think I wanted to tell my mom everything and have her tell me that it was okay, that I didn't have to have the abortion. But I couldn't tell her, and that never happened. I slept on the couch and got up the next morning and drove to the abortion clinic. I met the man who had fathered the baby; he went in and paid for the abortion and left, and I never saw him again.

They gave me a Tylenol 3; other than that, I had no pain medication. They took me to an operating room; I got up on the table, and they strapped my legs. The nurses talked to each other but ignored me like I wasn't a person. The doctor came in and didn't say a word to me. He told the nurses what to do. The pain was excruciating, and I started screaming. One of the nurses pinched my leg really hard, and said, "Think of the pain in the pinch instead of what is going on and quit screaming!" And then it was over. They took me into the back room where there were dirty mattresses on the floor, pushed against the walls. There were girls lying everywhere. I bled really badly, and the clinic workers determined that no one was with me, so they wouldn't let me leave because they were concerned about my driving. But finally they needed my mattress, so they pushed me out the back door.

When I got to my car, I had a flat tire. *Aw, come on! Give me a break!* I called AAA and sat down on the curb to wait. I was in terrible pain and bleeding. It was hot, and I was alone. I started crying, and I started praying. *God, You know what I just did. I know that You know me— thank You! I hope You can forgive me, and if You do, oh how I will thank You! But I know I will never forgive myself. If You hear me now, I need a friend.* As I sat on that curb, rocking back and forth and wailing for the loss of my son, God was with me. I felt His presence. *I don't know where I'll go from here, but I know that what just happened will change my life. I am asking that one day You will bring me a woman, just one woman, who I can tell what I went through so she won't do what I just did. And maybe I can forgive myself.*

The tow truck came and changed my tire, and I got in the car and drove home. I lay in bed and cried. I knew that I had been in the presence of God.

Because my blood type is O-negative, I have to have an Rh immune-globulin shot within seventy-two hours of giving birth. By law, I have to be notified of this, and the abortion clinic sent the notification to my house— and my husband got it. When I got home from work the next day, Tom handed it to me and asked, "Was it my child?"

I whispered, "No," and he left me. Rightfully so.

My life changed from that day, but not for the better. I worked at the same job another eight months. I sold my house and moved my son Christopher and me into a small apartment, went into a custody battle for him and nearly lost him. I started partying, met Phil, and ten months after the abortion, I got married again. Phil made me laugh and was a bad boy, and I thought that's what I deserved. I was drinking and partying, but I was never unfaithful again. Phil was an abuser, but I stayed. I knew that the God who held me on that curb was there, but I was so broken I couldn't reach Him.

I was twenty-nine and had no job. One month after we got married, Phil quit his job and we packed up my son and his daughter and moved to Oklahoma. It was the coldest winter they'd had since the turn of the century, with the wind chill factor sometimes as low as -17. There I was in Oklahoma, married to a man I didn't love. I knew no one and was totally lost. One Saturday night I was deep in despair and couldn't sleep, so I went out to the kitchen, crawled up onto the counter, put my feet in the sink and looked out the window. My anguish was overwhelming. Suddenly great sobs poured out of me. Misery and hopelessness had taken over my body.

Phil came out and asked what I was doing.

"I just need to be alone."

He mumbled, "Whatever" and went back to bed.

Dejected, I started praying. I knew at that moment that either something had to change or I wouldn't survive. I prayed all night with my feet in the sink, looking out the window at the stark, cold night and crying and praying and crying and asking God: *Where do I go from here? What should I do? How can I go on?* I finally pulled the phone book over to me and looked for a Catholic church. I found one in Moore, Oklahoma.

The next morning I went into the bedroom and told Phil I was going to church. He replied, "Don't wake up the kids," and turned back over.

I went to church for the first time in eight years, and it was very emotional. I shook and cried—I mean really cried, tears streaming down my cheeks. I sat on the next to the back row. There was a little old lady on my left and another little old lady on my right. I was longing to take the Eucharist but, because of my abortion, many affairs and divorce, I felt I shouldn't. The whole service was so overwhelming that I wanted to flee, but those two old ladies weren't budging! I looked for an escape but didn't think I should climb over the pews. So I held on, knowing that after communion it would be over and I could get out of there.

But after communion, Father George said, "Will everyone please be seated?"

Aw, come on! What now? I wanna get out of here! Everybody sat down, me included. "I want to introduce a lovely woman," Father George said. "Her name is Barbara Chisko, and she's here to tell you about her ministry."

Barbara stood up and explained, "I run a little pregnancy resource center in Oklahoma City. We reach out to women who are in crisis pregnancy, and we offer them alternatives to abortion." I wanted to laugh. I could almost hear God saying to me, "You told Me on that curb a year ago that you wanted Me to bring you one woman. I heard you, but I had to bring you to Oklahoma to do it. I let you spend the last year of your life royally screwing up. But now, here is the answer to your prayer." I suddenly felt a great peace. I went from bawling to smiling and giggling. I looked at those two little ladies and thought, *You are angels to keep me here!*

Instantly, I was back. I wanted everything. I wanted to go to confession. I wanted to participate in the Eucharist. I wanted to hug Father George. I wanted to love Barbara Chisko. I wanted to love the two angels next to me.

What I went through as a child made me who I am, and the abortion changed my life forever. In that little church in Oklahoma, I came back to Christ! I was born again. I now had a personal relationship with Jesus. I knew that I was going to survive!

I was the first person in line to talk to Barbara. "I just moved here. I don't know anything about Oklahoma. I don't even know where your center is, but I want to help. What can I do?"

"We're having volunteer training tonight," Barbara said.

"Tonight? Are you kidding me?"

That night I drove to the location; it was pitch black and I had no idea where I was going, but I finally found the huge house in downtown Oklahoma City. There were twenty-five other women there. The "volunteer training" turned out to be a prayer service; Barbara wisely didn't tell me that. During the evening, they asked, "Can we pray over you?"

I was raised in a home where we never prayed out loud, so I thought we'd all pray silently and remain in our seats. But before I knew it, I felt hands all over me—on my head and shoulders, on my knees and legs—and the ladies were praying for me out loud. At first I freaked out, but soon I relaxed and responded to the prayers that were being offered on my behalf. My life began again.

Those twenty-five women became my sisters in Christ, and they became my church. Barbara and I became friends, and she later told me that when she had looked into my eyes that morning at church, she had known. She was a charismatic Catholic, and she was so connected to God that she could look into my soul and know that I had lived a nightmare and had had an abortion. But I didn't open up and tell her for a long time.

I worked for four years in that crisis pregnancy center and helped many women. After two years I put my shame aside and finally started telling my story. Over the next months, my husband saw how God was changing my heart, and it piqued his interest; he became Catholic, and we were married in the Church. We made wonderful friends, and I had never been happier. My son Patrick was born there.

But then things fell apart and we lost everything. Phil got a job back in California. When I went to Barbara and told her that we were leaving, that I had to keep my family together, I thought she would say, "You can't! We need you!" But instead she asked, "Where are you going?" and when I said, "Mission Viejo," she responded, "Oh my gosh. There's a Birthright Center in Mission Viejo that is closing. God is calling you back to rescue that location and run it."

"Oh, no. I am not running a Birthright! I am not you. I just want to volunteer. I've answered God and have spent four years reaching out to women, and I feel like I'm done. I'm going back to open my own business and raise my kids." But God had a different plan.

I went back to California and became pregnant again with Conor, my youngest son. At the request of Barbara, Sue Jordan, the director of Birthright, tracked me down and asked me to go to a board meeting, which I did.

Phil wasn't working at that time, so I was doing day care—watching four small children along with my three. We didn't have anything, and I was getting our food from the food bank at our church. I became very active in the church and signed up for Cursillo, a marriage enrichment weekend, because I thought my husband needed to go. I was fine—or so I thought. If you know about Cursillo, you know that the first weekend is for the husband and the next is for the wife. Phil went, but I wasn't going to go; however, someone picked me up and took me the following Friday. The title of the weekend was "Sometimes God Doesn't Give You Options." I didn't give too much thought to the theme, but I came home on fire for the Lord.

But when I got home, I discovered a lot of boxes—like twelve or fifteen—on my front porch! There was also a white envelope with my name on it, so I opened it and found a note from Sue Jordan: "Kathleen, I have closed Birthright. I can't keep it going, but if anyone can make it work, you can. There's $34 in the bank. The lease wasn't paid, so there's no space. There is one volunteer, and I disconnected the phone. I moved the paperwork into your name. I'm moving to St. Louis. Good luck!"

I remembered Cursillo's leader, Father Ray, saying, "Sometimes God doesn't give you options," and I was so angry! Phil said, "Let's just put the boxes in the closet, and we'll pray about it." The next day I had four two-year-olds at my house at 6:00 a.m., and I was exhausted from the weekend and feeling tired and pregnant. Then the phone rang. The woman on the other end was screaming and crying hysterically. "My best friend is putting her daughter on an airplane tomorrow to go to Kansas to have a late term abortion!"

When I could get a word in I said, "Ma'am, I think you have the wrong number. What number did you call?"

"I called 364-3928." Sue didn't disconnect the Birthright phone; she had it forwarded to my home number! Sometimes God doesn't give you options! I had hungry babies in high chairs, I had a closet full of boxes from Birthright, and I had this screaming woman on the phone.

I had thought I was done, but sometimes God

doesn't give you options. I called the little girl's mother on the phone, and she cursed me to hell and damned me to Satan. "How dare you call me!" It was so horrible that I was shaking. Not knowing where to turn, I called my church and asked for prayer to prevent this wrong that was about to take place. As a result, a prayer service was planned that night to pray for the girl and to pray that her mother wouldn't send her to Kansas. I thought there might be a handful of people there, but instead it was standing room only. We named the baby Mary. The woman who initially called me called again the next day with the sad report that the mother had put her sixteen-year-old daughter on the plane to Kansas all by herself to end her six-month pregnancy.

That was it. I was convicted. I got the boxes out and changed the name from Birthright to Birth Choice and opened a pregnancy resource center. I rented a small space above Bubbles Bar in Mission Viejo because it was all I could afford; we shared the restroom with the women in the saloon.

That was the humble beginning of the ministry that today has eight fully licensed medical clinics in California with plans to expand throughout the country. Birth Choice is the premier licensed medical clinic battling Planned Parenthood nose-to-nose everyday. We can't take the option of abortion away, but what we can do is tell young people that they can choose life. Of the couples who come to our clinic who are headed to the abortion clinic, 77 percent change their minds and choose life! We give them information, support and medical services to equip them to parent or to consider adoption. God brings the people to our doors, and we help them.

We offer everything Planned Parenthood offers except abortion and contraception: well-woman care, prenatal care, STD testing and treatment, education, pregnancy ultra-sounds. Everything is free—no financial questions are asked. While we do have some volunteer nurses and nurse practitioners, most of our medical staff is paid. We help about 15,000 to 20,000 young people each year—some are in crisis pregnancies, some have had abortions, most are sexually active. We deal with the youth of today who are lost, who don't understand relationships, and who have found the pull of peer pressure to be stronger than their moral compass.

Along my journey, I went to a post-abortion Bible study group. Many of the women shared that they had gone back to the site of their abortion and prayed. So I asked my husband and sons if they would go with me, and together on a Saturday morning we went back to the abortion clinic where I had aborted my son. We stood outside the clinic, and my boys spiritually adopted their brother whom I named Tobias—Toby. We prayed the rosary and prayed with other people outside that clinic as abortions were being done inside. I cried because it was emotional, but I think my tears were more of joy because God had brought me so far from that broken woman who had sat on that curb. My boys later told me, "Mom, Toby was with us. We felt him."

I praised God that day. I praised Him for my family. It was that day that I asked my family for their blessing for me to share my story publicly. I had to ask because I knew I would be speaking in places where their friends and their friends' parents would be, so they had to be on board. And they were. That's when I started speaking, and I've had the privilege of speaking nationally.

I see now that I had to go to Oklahoma and meet Father George and Barbara Chisko and get introduced to Birthright and the pregnancy center movement—

and then I had to come back and play my role in California.

I reached out to God on that curb after my abortion; I leaned into Him and thanked Him that He was there. I reached out to God sitting on the counter with my feet in the sink in Oklahoma. I reached out to God at that tiny church. And I've never left Him since.

Kathleen didn't tell you, but I will: she is now one of the nation's leading anti-abortion advocates. In February 2010 Kathleen joined the 43rd President of the United States, George W. Bush, in receiving the acclaimed Cardinal John J. O'Connor Pro-Life Award for her distinguished achievement in the pro-life effort. In addition, she was named the 2011 Pro-life Person of the Year by the Diocese of Orange, and she works with a number of agencies including Focus on the Family in spreading the Birth Choice model.

Kathleen spent a lot of years in "Moab." In Kathleen's childhood she was poor, ridiculed and abused. She looked for security in men, in money and in her career. She failed at her marriage and hit an all-time low when she had the abortion, and then she made another bad choice in marrying a man she didn't love. But although Kathleen had left God, God never left Kathleen. He took her all the way to Oklahoma to get her attention and bring her back to Him. God completely restored her and turned her life into something beautiful for Him and His kingdom. Is this not an amazing story of God's redemption?

Remember Jesus' parable of the lost sheep from Matthew 18? Jesus tells the story of a shepherd who has one hundred sheep and one wanders away. He says the shepherd will leave the ninety-nine and go after the one, and when he finds the lost lamb, he'll be "happier about that one sheep than the ninety-nine that did not wander off" (18:13). Kathleen was that lost sheep that wandered off; Jesus went to get her and rejoiced to bring her back to the flock.

Do you know the song, "Tie a Yellow Ribbon Round the Old Oak Tree"? It tells the story of a prisoner who was just released and who was unsure if he would still be welcomed home by his family, so he wrote and told them to tie a yellow ribbon around the oak tree if they wanted him; he'd be on the bus and would just keep going if there wasn't a ribbon. When he got to the house, there wasn't one but one hundred yellow ribbons waving their welcome to him. I believe that, figuratively speaking, God has millions of oak trees with zillions of yellow ribbons waving their welcome to the Naomis and Kathleens of this world—and that includes you and me.

I'd like for you to read the lyrics from "When God Ran," a song from my *Mercies in Disguise* CD. The songwriters, J.P. Parenti and Benny Hester, beautifully express the truth of God's eagerness to welcome us back when we've strayed:

> Almighty God, the Great I Am,
> Immoveable Rock, Omnipotent, Powerful,
> Awesome Lord, Victorious Warrior,

Commanding King of Kings, Mighty Conqueror,
And the only time, the only time I ever saw Him run

Was when He ran to me,
Took me in His arms, held my head to His chest,
Said "My child's come home again."
Lifted my face, wiped the tears from my eyes.
With forgiveness in His voice
He said, "Child, do you know I still love you?"
It caught me by surprise when God ran.

The day I left home I knew I'd broken His heart.
I wondered then if things could ever be the same.
Then one night I remembered His love for me,
And down that dusty road ahead I could see…
It's the only time, the only time I ever saw Him run

Was when He ran to me,
Took me in His arms, held my head to His chest,
Said "My child's come home again"
Lifted my face, wiped the tears from my eyes
With forgiveness in His voice
He said "Child, do you know I still love you?"
It caught me by surprise when God ran.

No matter how long we've lived in Moab and what we've done, we're always welcome in God's house and at His table if we will acknowledge who He is and leave our Moab. Even when our circumstances are less than desirable, we can always praise God that He's a God of second chances.

4

Choosing to Praise God

IN TIMES OF WAITING

O NE of Dr. Seuss's most popular books is *Oh, the Places You'll Go!*[1] Catchy title, right? "Go!" brings positive connotations. Almost everybody likes to go! Go to the movies. Go on vacation. Go to the beach. Go for a hike or a swim or a run.

> Today is your day.
> You're off to Great Places!
> You're off and away!

Makes you want to jump right up and take off, doesn't it?

The book tells us that we can go in any direction we choose—"seeing great sights" and soaring to "high

---

1. Dr. Seuss, *Oh, the Places You'll Go!* Random House: New York, 1990, p. 12.

heights," but then possibly come down with an "unpleasant bump" and be in a "Slump." And then end up in the most useless place—"The Waiting Place."

No one wants to be in a waiting place, but we often are—waiting for the light to turn green, waiting to check out at the market, waiting in traffic to get to work, waiting to get a table at a restaurant. And then there's waiting to turn sixteen. Waiting to turn twenty-one. Waiting to get married. Waiting for that new job. Waiting to have a child. Waiting for that child to move out. Waiting to retire. Waiting to get a new car or a new house or a new couch or a new whatever it is you want so much. What are you waiting for to make you happy?

We wander around as though we're locked in some waiting room until some special something happens. Everyone just stands around, paralyzed with inertia, waiting for something to happen that will start life again. Life is on hold.

Sometimes our waiting is self-imposed, and sometimes it is thrust upon us. Trust me—I would not have chosen my time of waiting, but I can see now how God used it to deepen my trust in Him.

The first indication that something was wrong was during a time when I was flying a lot, speaking at various women's conferences and retreats across the country. About twenty minutes after take-off, I'd break out in a cold sweat. Very unusual. Because it happened more than once, I suspected something wasn't quite right, but I didn't know what.

My attendant first noticed a small red spot on my tailbone. A week later it broke open a little bit, like a little nick on your finger. We put antibiotic cream on it, but it wouldn't go away. Instead it began opening and growing larger until it was about the size of a pencil eraser. I had a wound nurse look at it, but she wasn't concerned.

Then I started experiencing the same cold sweats at various times during the day. Finally I asked my sister Denise, a nurse, to look at the spot and tell me what she thought. She didn't like the looks of it. She watched it for a few weeks and confirmed it wasn't getting any better.

Denise recommended that I have a doctor check it out, and after doing some research and finding a doctor who specialized in pressure wound care, Denise took me to my first appointment. I had to lie on my stomach on the table so the doctor could see the wound. (Another humbling moment when this very nice looking doctor walked in and greeted me with my bare bottom shining! Some things you never get used to.)

After close examination, Dr. Werner said, "I really, really hate to tell you this, but I need to open it up a little more so we can see what's going on underneath this one part of skin. I think there might be a little tunnel under this." That's the nature of pressure wounds; they tunnel, very much like ants in an ant farm. Dr. Werner opened it up about an inch and said, "I was afraid of this. There's a tunnel thing going on under here. I think we're going to have to do surgery to open it up to see how deeply it has tunneled." The thought of spending another night in a hospital was unnerving and frightening because it brought back horrible memories. But you do what you have to do.

After surgery I had a two-inch-deep wound all the way to my tailbone. Not the news I wanted, but what Dr. Werner did was rather fascinating. He used a wound vac to put negative pressure on the wound to help with drainage and to help increase blood flow, which expedites wound healing. He inserted a sponge into the wound, taped it down and cut a small hole in it that the vacuum hose would fit through. In other words, this contraption vacuumed my ant farm tunnel!

I couldn't continue sitting on that spot because sitting was what caused the damage in the first place. (I think the wound came from sitting so many hours on hard airplane seats; therefore, I now take my gel cushion from my wheelchair on flights to prevent that from happening again.) Dr. Werner sent me home to bed—indefinitely.

It was just before Thanksgiving that "the winter of my discontent" started. The doctor didn't tell me how long it would take; I don't think he knew, plus I think it was better for my mental health to take it one day at a time rather than to focus on the seemingly endless path that loomed before me. What I didn't know was that I would be stuck in bed for more than seven months.

I'm a firm believer that if you're fighting a war, it's wise to call on and seek counsel from an experienced veteran who has already fought that war, so I called my friend

Joni because she has personal experience with pressure wounds. Even though Dr. Werner had told me I could lay on my side, Joni said I'd heal faster if I lay on my stomach. I said, "I can't do that. I'll get claustrophobic on my stomach. I know I'll mentally wig out!"

But Joni persisted. "You can do it when you have to, so really try hard to push through and do it."

I called my physical therapist who happens not only to be my PT but also a former student of mine and now a friend. (I taught Kristin when she was in junior high. As a result of my injury, she became interested in physical therapy. She even drove me to some of my PT appointments while she was in high school so she could explore this career opportunity.) So I called Kristin and told her the situation. "Would you come to my home and help me get comfortable on my stomach so I won't freak out being face down?" She came and brought a wedge with a hole in it for my face. She stood over me on the bed with her feet beside my hips, quickly rolled me onto my stomach and, at the same time, lifted my shoulders so my attendant could slide the wedge under me. It worked. I was so excited! It had been fourteen years since I had been on my stomach. It felt so good! Before my injury, I had always been a stomach sleeper; so I thought this would work. However, after an hour or two of having nothing to look at but the sheet under my face, I became bored beyond imagination. I listened to books on tape and music, but there was no escaping it—I was going crazy with inactivity and the absence of visual stimulation.

Something had to be done, so Kristin devised a way to wedge a pillow under one side of my tummy and shoulder, just enough that my face could turn sideways. Yea, fresh air! I was still on my tummy, but not so flat that my face was buried. This way, I could see the people who came into my room and talk to them. When I was facing right, I could watch TV. When my neck would get tired of that position, my attendant would turn me to the other side where I could see out our picture window to the backyard. We have a very pretty jacaranda tree, and I remember praising God for Mike Imlay who landscaped our backyard and placed that jacaranda right where I could see it. With the slightest breeze, the leaves would flutter ever so gracefully.

Scripture says, "Be still, and know that I am God" (Ps. 46:10). When we're still, it's amazing how much we see—really see—to be thankful for. Our daily busyness is often an obstacle to appreciating God's creation, His watchful care over us and His provision for us. One of the lessons I learned from my "waiting place" was to take time to notice special things around me, to appreciate things that might otherwise have gone unnoticed.

One morning I hit the switch on my adaptive phone on my pillow with my chin, which dialed the operator. I said, "Special Services," which told her that I am disabled and needed assistance to make the call. I gave her Mike Imlay's number to dial for me. He didn't answer, so I left a message and said, "Mike, I just want you to know that I'm so grateful that years ago you planted that jacaranda tree in just the right spot for me to enjoy while I'm stuck here in bed." It's funny—when I was up and running around, I never would have taken the time to pick up the phone and let him know how that beautiful tree brought joy to my life.

After a few weeks I hit a wall. I couldn't stand it any longer; the walls of my bedroom were closing in on me and I felt like I was suffocating. I called Joni again.

"I'm going down!" I admitted. "I've watched every romantic comedy that Blockbuster has on the shelf, people have come and read Scripture to me, I've listened to books on tape until I can no longer stay focused. I'm drowning in monotony. Got any advice? Anything new?"

Joni replied, "Renée, when I was in bed with a pressure wound, memorizing Scripture and hymns was lifesaving. Have someone write a Scripture or a verse to a hymn on a 3x5 card and put it on a bulletin board by your bed. If you don't have one, get one. And every time you open your eyes, focus on it."

So I did. I started with Philippians 4:8: "Whatever is true, whatever is noble, whatever is right, whatever is pure, whatever is lovely, whatever is admirable—if anything is excellent or praiseworthy—think about such things."

I not only memorized it, I meditated on it, just like the Scripture instructed. I had plenty of time! I picked the first word—true. *What's true in my life? God led me to a good doctor who's directing me to do what I need to do to get this thing healed properly. That's true. My sister*

Denise is a nurse and lives just behind me so she can come every day and change the dressing on my wound. That's true, and that's good. What is noble? That's kind of a funky word. Don't hear too much of it these days. Mike—what a noble, amazing man to put up with me. Thank you, Lord. What is pure? The smell of the tangerine my attendant peeled by my bed before she popped the slices into my mouth. What a clean, pure smell. Daniel's angelic, innocent smile that lights up my heart. That's pure. Jesus. The ultimate example of purity, taking the nails for me. Nothing is more pure than His love.

One day after I'd been meditating on Philippians 4:8, I looked over and saw my empty wheelchair sitting by the closet. Never had I had warm, fuzzy thoughts about my wheelchair. It was not a vehicle of freedom but a symbol of my imprisonment. But suddenly I saw it in a different light, and I said out loud, "Well, hello, old friend. Sure wish I could hang out with you today." I laughed when I heard my own words. If you had told me years ago that I would ever call my wheelchair "friend," I would have said, "Yeah, right." Yet here I am.

I was learning that God's Word changes our heart, our heart influences our mind, and our mind controls our attitude. My feelings toward my wheelchair had changed. No longer was it my enemy; now it was my companion. No longer was it my cell of captivity; now it was my agent of freedom.

Another Scripture that ministered to me was Psalm 57:1:

> Have mercy on me, O God, have mercy on me,
>   for in you my soul takes refuge.
> I will take refuge in the shadow of your wings
>   until the disaster has passed.

As a Catholic, I was very familiar with this verse because the penitential rite in the Mass almost always includes, "Lord have mercy; Christ have mercy; Lord have mercy." I had recited that prayer all my life. As a cantor at Mass, how many times had I sung "On Eagles' Wings"? But when I chose to memorize this Scripture, the last phrase jumped off the page: "I will take refuge in the shadow of your wings *until the disaster has passed.*" That meant that what I was going through was going to come to an end! God encouraged me that my ordeal was not going to last forever; one day I would get out of that bed! There was reason to praise Him—for His promise and for communicating this hope to me!

As Joni suggested, I memorized hymns. I found there to be such power, such praise, such eloquence in the wonderful old hymns of the church. "Jesus, the Very Thought of Thee" brought me to a place of thinking about Jesus— the life He led and the death He died for us, for me.

Being a musician, I'm always interested to know the moment that inspired the writing of a great song. One of the most moving stories behind the writing of a hymn comes from "It Is Well with My Soul." The story is now widely known—how Horatio Spafford, who had lost a son in 1871 and then was in financial ruin after the Great Chicago Fire, put his wife and four daughters on a ship bound for England in 1873 but was himself delayed by business. He planned to join them shortly; however, their ship sank, and his wife alone survived. On his way to join his wife, Horatio penned the words to this great hymn as he passed near the spot where their ship had gone down.

> When peace like a river attendeth my way,
> When sorrows like sea billows roll.
> Whatever my lot, Thou hast taught me to say,
> It is well; it is well with my soul.

Wow. Mr. Spafford's loss made my confinement seem insignificant by comparison. As I meditated on the words to the song, I reflected on the story behind it. I was inspired and impressed that Mr. Spafford could feel such peace in the midst of his unspeakable grief. Although I'll never know for sure, my guess is that he wrote that song as a sacrifice of praise to God—not that he felt like it but that he disciplined himself to react in submission to God. What a remarkable man. What a beautiful hymn. Later I learned that Horatio and his wife had had three more children, including a son who died in infancy. (Are you counting? That's six children they'd lost!) They moved with their remaining two daughters to Jerusalem and helped found the American Colony, an organization that served the poor.

Another great hymn is "How Great Thou Art": "When I consider all the worlds Thy hands have made. . . .Then sings my soul . . . how great Thou art!" Just thinking about how God, the creator of the universe, hung galaxies in space light years away and also designed beautiful, delicate flowers that open in a spectacle of unparalleled brilliance—beauty He designed for us to enjoy. I think He probably hoped that when we observed these natural wonders that we would recognize that He put them here for us.

While lying there in bed, I began to identify with the Israelites and their waiting experience. Forty years of aimless wandering. Their wilderness experience was their own fault. They sent spies into the Promised Land to check it out. Notice the term "Promised Land"—so-called because God promised it to them. You can't get any more certain or secure than that. Yet they sent twelve spies in to check it out, and the spies came back scared out of their wits. "There are giants in there!" ten of them reported. (You can read about it in Numbers 14.) Although God had proven Himself faithful time and time again, the people believed the skeptical spies instead of trusting God and His promises. They relied on the words of men and their own logic instead of remembering God's loyalty. They ran on fear instead of faith. They took their eyes off God and looked at the situation. They focused on their circumstances instead of God's commitment.

This wasn't their first mistake. Remember that these same Israelites had used their gold to construct a golden calf to worship while Moses was on Mount Sinai receiving the Ten Commandments from God. God had miraculously rescued them from a life of slavery, manual labor and oppression. If sending all the plagues wasn't evidence enough that God was at work, He also performed the Red Sea miracle. (The Israelites crossed the sea on dry ground, but the pursuing Egyptian army perished when the wall of water crashed in on them.) Yet on the way to Mount Sinai, they grumbled and griped. They were in that waiting place in between their circumstance and their promise. Uncertainty loomed ahead, and hardship was their shadow. So they threw a pity party. "We're going to starve to death!" "We're tired!" And the one that really frosts me, "We were better off back in Egypt!"! Imagine God's ire. I'm glad He's a holy God because if it had been me, I would have been royally ticked off at their ingratitude and lack of faith.

But God still gave them manna every day. What is manna? The Israelites asked the same question. The literal translation of "manna" is "what is it?" It was something nourishing that God designed and provided just for them every morning. But here's the catch: He gave them just enough for each day, and He told them clearly to gather just enough for their family for one day. Some didn't trust that there would be more tomorrow, so they gathered more. And guess what? The next day, the manna from the previous day stunk and was filled with maggots! Yuck!

So what did that say to me there in my bed? I, like the Israelites, was in the wilderness. Aimless. Purposeless. Feeling the unfairness of it all. I felt like I had a

right to be frustrated. Being paralyzed should be affliction enough, but then to be confined to bed? Come on,
already! But God gave the Israelites manna for each day,
and I began to see that He gave me manna for each day
as well. Someone has said, "God doesn't give us grace
today for tomorrow's struggles." Scripture says, "Therefore do not worry about tomorrow, for tomorrow will
worry about itself. Each day has enough trouble of its
own" (Matt. 6:34). No use to worry about how long this
was going to take. I just had to get through each day.

I began to realize that God gave me, like the Israelites, manna every day. He gave me a son who came
home after school, jumped on my bed and told me about
his day. (Oh how I looked forward to hearing him come
through the door!) He also gave me an understanding
husband who didn't get impatient or frustrated at having his already paralyzed wife now bedridden for several
months. It couldn't have been an enjoyable time for him,
but he came in with a smile every single day. God gave
me family to support us emotionally and to take care of
various physical tasks. He gave me friends to call and
stop by to visit. He gave me that jacaranda tree to enjoy.
He taught me to love Scripture as never before and to
sing the hymns of faith with new appreciation and gusto.
Whatsoever things are praiseworthy, think on these things.
Manna from heaven every day.

I was in my Dr. Seuss "Waiting Place" for seven and
a half months—from just before Thanksgiving until July
4. How appropriate that America's Independence Day

was the day I was released and set free. I was off to "great places," or Hume Lake in the Sequoia National Forest to be exact. Just before my confinement, we had purchased a "gently used" handicapped-accessible motor home. We picked it up in Albuquerque, New Mexico, when I was there speaking for a Women of Virtue conference, and drove it home. Two weeks later, I was diagnosed with the pressure wound, so it sat for eight months. The day I was released I rolled out of the bedroom and into the motor home, and off we went—Mike, Daniel, me and my wheelchair, or my *adventuremobile*. (Remember, God's Word changes our heart, our heart influences our mind, and our mind controls our attitude.)

There are many life lessons in Dr. Seuss's *Oh, the Places You'll Go*. And actually a little theology as well. Sometimes life takes us to the heights of adventure and sometimes to the dark valley or, maybe hardest to handle, to the dungeon of the dreaded waiting place. No matter where life takes us and where God allows us to go, we cannot escape His love. Wherever we fly or flop, God is there to love us and scoop us up in His arms. I've learned that it's often in these difficult, seemingly useless waiting-place periods of my life that God can get my attention and teach me powerful lessons.

5

Choosing to Praise God

WHEN THINGS GO FROM BAD TO WORSE

GIDEON knew firsthand about things going from bad to worse. He was a lowly man, minding his own business, when he was suddenly catapulted from obscurity to the role of an army commander. He was unqualified for his position and fighting a war that was, by all indications, doomed to failure. Disaster and defeat appeared certain. What was God up to? Here's the story. (You can read it in its entirety in Judges 6–7.)

Because of the Israelites' sin and because they had turned to Baal, a false god, the Lord had allowed the Midianites to invade and ravage the Israelites' land. Whenever the Israelites planted crops, the ruthless Midianites came in at harvest time like a swarm of locusts, stealing their crops and destroying their livestock. Not surprisingly, the Israelites cried out to God for help, and

God, in His faithfulness and love for His people, answered.

Gideon was hiding out, threshing wheat in a winepress, rather than the usual method of threshing the wheat out in the open where the wind could carry the useless chaff away. By using the winepress, he could be out of sight so that the Midianites would not see him and come steal the grain. While he was working, an angel of the Lord—according to Bible scholars, Jesus Himself—appeared to him and said, "The Lord is with you, mighty warrior" (6:12). I can just see Gideon turning and looking behind him to see whom the angel was calling "mighty warrior." *Who, me? You're talking to me?* Gideon certainly didn't qualify to be a warrior, much less a mighty one. He told the angel that his clan was the weakest clan and that he was the weakest in his family. In other words, he said, "You must have me confused with someone else."

But Gideon's protests did not change the angel's mind. He told Gideon that he had been chosen to save the Israelites from the Midianites. This is reminiscent of when the Lord called out to Moses from the burning bush and instructed him to rescue the Israelites from slavery in Egypt. Gideon felt as ill-equipped as Moses did and protested in much the same way. And just as in the situation with Moses, the angel reassured Gideon that the Lord would be with him and would give him victory in defeating the Midianites. In addition, He reassured Gideon that he would not die.

Now here's a key point. When Gideon recognized that he had actually been talking to an angel of the Lord, he built an altar to God and called it "The Lord of Peace." Gideon didn't have to build an altar. He must have done so because he wanted to pay tribute to the God who cared enough to appear to him. Building the altar reveals Gideon's heart; he took time to worship the one true God.

Gideon's first task as the Lord's warrior was to tear down his father's shrine to the false god Baal and to erect an altar to God in its place—a move that would definitely anger the Baal worshipers. Gideon did as he was instructed, and the next morning when the people woke up, they saw that the monument to Baal had been demolished, and there in its place was the altar Gideon had built to the Lord. What's more, there before them was Gideon with a bull he had sacrificed on the newly built altar. God used Gideon to make a statement: "I am the Lord, the one true God who brought you out of Egypt. I am the One who is worthy of your praise, and I will not bless you as long as you are worshiping other gods."

Baal's worshipers were furious and wanted Gideon put to death. However, Gideon's father stepped in and proclaimed that if Baal had actually been God, he could defend himself. Redeeming statement, don't you think? Woo-hoo to Gideon's dad for coming around! Gideon lived, and I'll bet his faith and trust in the Lord grew.

About that same time the armies of Midian and other eastern tribes joined forces, crossed the Jordan and settled in the Valley of Jezreel just east of the river. Gideon sent word to the other tribes of Israel to come and form an army. The vastness of the Midianite army understandably had Gideon feeling overwhelmed, so just to make sure he was hearing God correctly, he asked for a sign: "If you will save Israel by my hand as you have promised—look, I will place a wool fleece on the threshing floor. If there is dew only on the fleece and all the ground is dry, then I will know that you will save Israel by my hand as you said" (6:37). (Notice that? Gideon knew that God said it, but he still didn't quite believe it.) The next morning the fleece was so wet that Gideon rang a bowlful of water out of it, but the ground around it was dry. Unmistakably, God had responded to Gideon's need for reassurance.

That should have been enough, but it wasn't. Gideon still required more, so he told God that he needed just a little more proof. "This time make the fleece dry and the ground covered with dew" (6:39). God did it, just as Gideon had specified. I love how patient God was with Gideon.

So Gideon gathered his troops and formed an army of thirty-two thousand men. Unfortunately, the Midianite army was four times larger. Things looked hopeless. Then God told Gideon, "In order that Israel may not boast against me that her own strength has saved her, announce now to the people, 'Anyone who trembles with fear may turn back and leave Mount Gilead'" (7:2–3). Two-thirds of the army went home; only ten thousand remained. By all logic victory was impossible. The odds were now about 13:1. Could things get any worse? Apparently yes.

The Lord then said to Gideon, "There are still too many men." *What?!* "Take them down to the water to drink and I will sift them for you there. Separate those who lap the water with their tongues like a dog from those who kneel down to drink" (7:5). Only three hundred knelt down to drink, and God said, "With the three hundred men that lapped I will save you and give the Midianites into your hands. Let all the other men go, each to his own place" (7:7). Gideon dismissed seven thousand and seven hundred more, so now his army was reduced to three hundred men! The odds were now about 450:1. Things were about as bad as they could get. Apart from God, winning was completely out of the question.

I wonder how Gideon felt. He was trusting God, but let's be realistic. Victory had looked hopeless at the start with 4:1 odds. Then they went 13:1, and now they were 450:1! Talk about things going from bad to worse! Nobody could win being outnumbered that badly. Defeat was imminent and embarrassment was inevitable. But praise the Lord; He's not limited by our reality. There's only one way that an army of three hundred could defeat an army over one hundred times its size: God had to do it. And that's exactly what God wanted the Israelites and you and me to see!

Gideon moved the army of three hundred to the hill above the Midianite camp. There were so many Midianites that Scripture says they were "thick as locusts," and they had so many camels that they couldn't be counted. Before the Israelites attacked, God instructed Gideon to sneak down at night into the enemy camp and listen to a conversation. Gideon arrived just as an enemy soldier was telling a friend his dream. The friend interpreted the dream as this: "This can be nothing other than the sword of Gideon, son of Joash, the Israelite. God has given the Midianites and the whole camp into his hands" (7:14).

When Gideon heard this, he worshiped the Lord. I believe that Gideon's heart to worship God is what made him a mighty warrior. God didn't choose a military hero or a political leader of the Israelites; He chose insignificant, obscure Gideon who really wasn't all that brave or full of faith. Yet he worshiped God, and God knew Gideon's heart for Him and saw his potential.

Gideon went running back up the hill to the camp. "Get up!" he shouted. "The Lord has given the Midianite camp into your hands" (7:15). Gideon obeyed the Lord's directions and divided his army of three hundred into three groups. He gave each soldier a trumpet and an empty jar with a torch inside and spread them out on the hill above the enemy camp. When Gideon gave the command, they blew their trumpets all at once and broke their jars so that the torches suddenly blazed, piercing the darkness. Then all three hundred men shouted as loudly as they could, "For the Lord and for Gideon!" (7:18) Then they continued to blow their trumpets like crazy.

The Midianites, startled out of their sleep by the shouting and horns, and seeing all the torches, thought they were being attacked by a huge army. They went crying and running like proverbial chickens with their heads cut off. They actually turned and fought each other with their swords! What was left of the army fled and was eventually over taken by the men that Gideon had previously sent home. The Midianites were wiped out, and the Israelites were freed from oppression. Who could doubt that this was done by the hand of God?

One of the fascinating things about this story is that the situation was bad enough at the start and then seemingly went from bad to worse. Have you ever had this happen to you? You pray for something in faith, believing it will get better, and instead it just gets worse? Maybe you're praying for a health issue, and instead of recovering, the person gets more ill. Perhaps you're praying for a new job, and you're only met with dead ends. Or it could be that you are having increasingly upsetting relationship conflicts. You intensify your prayer efforts, and the situation seems to go downhill. Invariably you ask God, "What's up with this? I prayed, believing, and nothing good is happening. Are You listening? Do You care?"

I feel that sometimes God allows a situation to appear hopeless so that, when things turn around, we recognize His hand in orchestrating the process as well as the outcome. He's always at work in our behalf, and Scripture reminds us that the Lord wants you and me to be aware that He is working His plan in our lives. He doesn't want us to shrug our shoulders and say, "Well, that was lucky," or "Looks like things worked out after all." No! I believe He wants us to see His faithfulness and acknowledge His involvement in our lives. In doing so we learn to trust Him more, and as a result, we have a more intimate relationship with Him.

We walked with our dear friend Stewart Fischer through such a situation. Here is his story in his own words:

> I've enjoyed my career in management in the franchise restaurant business, and over the years, I've secured high-level positions in product marketing, franchising and new restaurant development. I was the chief operating officer in a family business, but unfortunately, over time it became clear that this family had issues with each other. But being an optimist by nature, I assumed that all the successful things we were accomplishing in the business would create job stability for me. I was wrong. The biblical truth that a "house divided within will not stand," became a reality, and in May 2009, at the age of forty-two, married and with two young daughters, I found myself unemployed.

> I wasn't all that worried; after all, past experience told me that I'd be employed again and quickly. I had been between jobs before, but I had always found a new position within a few months. It was just a matter of doing my legwork and finding the position that was right for

me. Fortunately, we had a large nest egg from the sale of our previous home, and we could draw on that in the interim. Little did I know then that this "interim" would turn into almost two years, leaving us with a three-month reserve before we were literally out on the streets.

For about four months I worked with a friend of mine who was launching a new company. Because it was new, I did a lot of pro bono work for him with a three-pronged hope for return: first, I wanted to help my friend; second, I expected and hoped that my services would lead to a full-time position as the company took off; and third, I must admit, there was comfort in knowing I had a place to be productive and a purpose for waking up in the morning.

But this arrangement caused friction between my wife and me. Ann, being more pragmatic, felt that I should not be working for nothing but rather should be taking the time to look for a job. "Ann, be patient; it's going to happen. Something will materialize," I would tell her. But I saw Ann in turmoil, recognizing the need to trust and support her husband while trying hard to subordinate her own fears and concerns about the unknown future.

I was depending on the longterm, trusting that things would pan out, whereas she was looking at the immediate. "Our savings are dwindling and we shouldn't disrupt the girls' lives and their school," she frequently reminded me, which I wholeheartedly agreed with. (When I was working, we had decided to sacrifice to provide our two daughters with a Catholic school education.) Our savings account, which we planned to use as a down payment for the purchase of our next home, was being used for our daily expenses, and it was dwindling fast.

I'm a "the glass is half full" person, and Ann is "the

glass is half empty"—or at least she's a lot more pragmatic. Usually that's helpful in a marriage. If both look at the glass as half full, then no one would see warning signs. If both see the glass as half empty, then neither would smell the flowers and see the beauty. But our differences in this situation frustrated both of us; I was much too optimistic and casual for her comfort, and she was too demanding and fearful for mine. During this time of uncertainty, there was a full-fledged tug-of-war between us. I worked on convincing myself and her that I had a plan and was in control, but as the reality of joblessness persisted, I avoided broaching the subject with Ann at all because I had nothing concrete or reassuring to share with her. This avoidance and lack of dialogue only exacerbated Ann's lack of confidence in me.

Around July we decided to get away from our stress, so we took our annual trip to Montana to my in-laws' lake home. However attractive leaving our stress behind sounded, we were kidding ourselves. I was very demoralized as a man. I found that I couldn't make simple decisions such as pulling into the next gas station to refuel without Ann's input. She was frustrated with my indecisiveness as well as my joblessness. We both tried very hard to keep the stress and anxiety away from our girls but with little success. The tension rode with us every minute of every day, with emotional outbursts spewing out between Ann, me and the girls all too frequently. Whether we were talking about it or not, my joblessness loomed over us like a dark, threatening cloud.

The rubber had met the road, and it was time for me to look at the start-up business differently. When we returned from Montana, I went to my friend and told him that I could no longer continue doing pro bono work; I had to look after my family and devote every minute of my time to looking for a paying job. The company wanted to hire me, but they simply did not have the capital to put me on the payroll.

So now we were into the fall and looking at six months of unemployment. Ann was still on me, frustrated by how much time I had spent helping my friend when I could have been looking for a job. I retaliated that there is some risk involved—that I had to take a risk in order to try to build something. She tried to keep her frustration in, but it was beginning to be too much for my sweet wife.

My sense of worthlessness was exacerbated in watching my two girls get ready for school each day and Ann get ready for her part-time job while I stood there in my pajamas, teeth not brushed, not showered, and with nowhere to go—a reminder that I had no purpose other than the same rigmarole of job searching on the Internet, opening my e-mail only to find constant silence from recruiters and to see that contacts were not getting back to me as promised. (Believe it or not, receiving rejection letters was actually preferable to the too frequent nonreply. At least a rejection letter provided closure, giving me freedom to focus somewhere else.)

Sometimes Ann would come home for lunch for some "us time." She would gently ask how my day was going and probe into my morning activities, only to find out the reality of zero progress. Frustrated with what appeared to be my laziness, Ann would try to offer ideas and other suggestions, which were not well received by me, and we would end up in an argument, ultimately leaving her and me emotionally undone. I not only felt rejected by the job market; I also felt rejected by my wife. Both indicated that I was a failure. "You are defeating me, making it very difficult for me to sound positive and marketable when you've just chewed me out and assured me that even you have no confidence in me," I would tell her.

Please know that I'm not being critical of Ann. She's a loving wife and a smart, caring mother. She and I enjoy a happy marriage and a loving relationship, centered on God. We strive to do what it takes to support each other; she has always supported me in my decisions. Our friction was caused by the bleak situation and the constant pressure we were under. It was very tough for both of us, maybe even harder for her than me. I at least was busy exploring every possible tip and avenue and was using every ounce of energy I had to look for a job, but she was helpless to do anything to speed the process, and she did not know every detail of my thoughts and activities. I understood her frustration, but at the time, it didn't help.

If you want to learn patience, one of the fruits of the Spirit (Gal. 5:22), a job search will do it! I was sending out résumés, tracking down leads and working with recruiters. People would tell me, "I'll get back to you," and then I'd wait for their reply. Sometimes it would take several days and sometimes it would never come at all. When you're desperate and counting on people to follow up, minutes feel like hours, a day feels like a week, a week feels like a month, and a month feels like a year. A few times I got what appeared to be strong leads that looked very promising, and the company would show interest. The "courtship" would sometimes take two or three months and then eventually fizzle out. It was an endless vortex of hope and then disappointment, expectation followed by failure. It was absolutely excruciating! Having to tell my family that the job prospect did not come to fruition was like having to tell them I was being laid-off again and again. I would think that I was seeing the light at the end of the tunnel, but it would turn out to be another freight train coming my way.

Friends helped when they could. One friend was starting a video résumé business. He usually charged $600 to $1,000 to do a video résumé, but because he was a close friend and wanted to help, he offered to do mine at no charge. So I drove up to Hollywood to his studio, complete with camera equipment, lights and makeup. We had thoroughly prepared the script, but just as we were ready to start the film rolling, my cell phone rang. "Stewart!" I heard Ann's hysterical voice. "I just got a phone call from school. Elizabeth [my eighth-grade daughter] is unconscious on the playground! The ambulance is on the way, and I'm racing to the school."

At that moment, I realized that absolutely nothing mattered except my family. Losing the house, losing the cars, losing the private school—nothing was important compared to my daughter's health. Heading down the freeway through LA traffic—which, by the way, lives up to every horror story you've ever heard—I drove as fast as I dared, but it still took about two hours to drive from Hollywood to the hospital in Mission Viejo. During that long, arduous drive, I prayed and cried my heart out, asking God, "What is going on? What are You trying to tell me? Why are You doing this to me?!"

When at last I arrived, I saw Elizabeth. She was all banged up, but she was alive and talking. After a myriad of tests, we were told that she has epilepsy and had had a grand mall seizure. Once we knew the diagnosis, we realized that she had already shown signs; Elizabeth had been having approximately five to six silent seizures (or check outs) a day that we had mistaken for simply not paying attention. We had not understood why her grades had been suffering for almost a year. In hindsight, I could only imagine that she must, due to her poor grades, have felt the same feeling of inadequacy as her daddy did with his inability to provide for the family in finding a job. We started new regimens to find the right medications to control her seizures, but there were side effects like weight gain and lethargy. Some of the meds didn't work or made her very sick, and others changed Elizabeth's personality. The fact that we had private insurance with a very high deductible did not matter to us; our quest to control and eliminate Elizabeth's seizures took priority. But all the expensive tests and treatments were not working.

By one of God's "coincidences," Renée told Ann about a doctor who designs diets based on blood type; his medical specialty is "applied kinesiology." Ann drove Renée to one of her appointments with Dr. Vrzal and took the opportunity to check out what he does and to ask him questions. We decided to give it a try, and to make a long story short, it worked! We are now able to control Elizabeth's seizures with her diet—praise the Lord! The whole process took about three months, but it felt like it took forever.

Looking back, the ordeal with Elizabeth actually helped my relationship with my wife Ann. Since we had been under so much stress, I think we had forgotten how to pull together. We both had the same goal in mind but different ideas on how to accomplish that goal. But when our daughter became ill, we relearned how to work together and draw on each other for strength and understanding. It was an important breakthrough.

By then I had been out of work for just under a year. Somewhere in the process I started keeping a quiet time with the Lord every morning, reading the Word and praying. That's what really kept me afloat. I read the book of Job and marveled at how he could stay so focused on God when his world was crumbling around him. Job's courage gave me strength and hope, but I still felt discouraged and confused at times. I used my morning quiet times to renew my mind, to focus on good things and to praise God for them. I was learning to trust in Him. I'd pray, *Thank You, Lord, for Ann, that she's hanging in there with me. Thank You that she's willing to work part-time to help out and that You gave her a job. Thank You, God, for the equity in our previous home that gave us a nest egg to fall back on. I praise You for my two precious daughters and that they are good girls—respectful, polite, intelligent and not into the pitfalls of adolescence like attitude and drugs. Thank You, Father, for Your presence with us. Thank You that I can trust and know that the answer is on the way.* These times of finding things to be thankful for kept me from focusing on my trials and transformed and refreshed my mind.

I really needed these times of renewal with the Lord, because life out there didn't get any easier; in fact the longer my joblessness lingered, the harder it got. When you go through tough times, you learn many lessons. We began to understand that some people naturally shy away from those who are struggling or hurting because they often do not know what to say or how to react. Some do not want to hear about your trouble, maybe because they fear that it might inconvenience them or because it might make them feel guilty about their own happiness. I was surprised to see that those who had much to give had very little to offer, and those who had little gave much.

For example, a dear lifetime friend observed and commented to me that Ann looked horribly tired and worn out. Then he began telling me how great his company was doing, that they had increased business by 200 to 300 percent and needed to hire two hundred additional people to help with production. I managed to be happy for him, but I think you'll understand that it was hard to hear in my situation. He's a great guy and a good family man, but he seemed insensitive and clueless as to how what he was saying was being received.

I opened up to a family member about how tough it was to be between jobs and looking for employment. He interrupted that he understood because his teenager was having difficulty finding a summer job. Suddenly the attention was turned back on him and his family—plus it was hurtful in my crisis of doing everything I could to support and take care of my family to be compared to a kid who wanted a part-time job for spending money! These are people my family cares about, and I know they care about us, but I've come to realize that when things are going well in peoples' lives, it can be hard to relate to others who are suffering. God sends us challenges to soften our hearts—to make us less self-absorbed and more considerate of others.

Distraught by my inability to get a job and disillusioned by human failings, I spent time with a dear spiritual mentor, Father Leo Celano. I poured my heart out to him and we prayed together; then he gave me perspective: "Never put anyone on a pedestal. Only God deserves to be on a pedestal. People are human, and they will fail you." He gently reminded me that we are all dancing on broken legs. But God never fails! *Thank You, Lord, that You never fail, that You will never let me down.*

Let me quickly add that some whom I least expected to share and who had nothing to gain showed agape love. Some friends and family stood with us through the entire ordeal. Some of the best ministering was by those who would simply ask, "How's it going, and how are you doing?" and then just listen, really listen. They invited us for dinner or out to movies or concerts. They offered help. They prayed with us and for us. But, most importantly, they showed by their words and their actions that they really cared. I can't begin to tell you how important their support was to us. We will forever be grateful for their true friendship.

Then it came. Late in November of 2010, I was referred to Ken, a restaurant hospitality recruiter. He told me about a particular regional chain of sixty-nine restaurants that was looking for a director of company operations. They had been trying to fill the position for several months but had not found the right person. I remember praying to God, *If it is Your will . . .* In meeting with the executive team and owners through the interviewing process, I discovered that we held similar views about life and people and about how to build a sustainable business.

In January, 2010, the recruiter who was handling the negotiations called. When I answered the phone, he said, "Well, congratulations, Stewart. You got the job. They went for everything we asked for."

I was, of course, home alone. Ann was at work and the girls were at school. My first reaction was total disbelief that it was over. After almost two years of frustration, disappointments, trying to remain hopeful when everything looked hopeless, I had a job! Then I felt that incredible pressure being lifted. I needed a drum roll! I needed an orchestra to play "The Hallelujah Chorus"! I stood there and thought, *Is this really happening?* Back and forth between disbelief and relief.

I had to share the news, so I called Ann and said, "The recruiter just called. I got the job! Can you believe it? And they gave me everything I asked for!"

That night at dinner Ann and I announced to the girls that I had been offered a job and had accepted. To my delight, Ann and the girls sprang up from the table, and we found ourselves hugging and jumping like little kids in a playground. I savored every moment with great pleasure. That night Ann and I vowed never to forget how this ordeal and its storms had transformed us as a family. We joked that we would remember what we had learned from this experience because we were not interested in a "refresher course of humility and grace" from God!

Waking up on that Monday, January 17, I felt very different than on other Mondays. I had a purpose and a spring in my step; I was going to work! On my way I prayed very hard, thanking God for all His blessings—including the ones that are difficult to understand. I vowed to God that I would take this hour-long morning drive and praise His name in prayer every day on my way to work. This is a promise I have kept and continue today. I came home that January night after a long first day at work to find my beautiful wife and daughters waiting for me with a candle-lit dinner ready on the table. What a rich and lucky man I am!

Ten months into the job, things are going strong. During this economical downturn, the business is doing well, and my team is motivated and achieving great success. I recently had dinner with the owner of the company, and he told me that he was pleased with my work and wanted to be sure I was happy in my role in the company. He proceeded to share that he would like to see his next executive come from operations and that he could see that person being me! Who would have thought this conversation would happen less than a year into my affiliation with the company? Suddenly, it is my dream job! God is faithful.

In going through job loss and Elizabeth's physical concerns, I learned that only complete surrender to God brings peace. He's in charge. I'm not. I learned that the tougher the challenge, the sweeter the fruit. A Dutch proverb says, "A gem cannot be polished without friction, nor a man perfected without trials." I learned how to have a thankful heart and to give glory to God, even during trials. I hope to always remember how important it is to follow up on promises I make so as not to leave people hanging. And I will forever be more sensitive to other people's pain and struggle.

Father Leo told me, "God's plan is perfect but not necessarily easy." Stanford Coggins, a very grounded Christian friend of mine, sent me an e-mail with these words: "Congratulations, Stewart. Praise God for the challenges and praise Him for the amazing impact you will have on people for having brushed against this adversity for so long. Nothing will go wasted. I pray God uses your courage, endurance, perseverance and poise to your credit for the benefit of others and to His glory!"

I pray that this is true in my life, both today and forever.

Mike and I rejoice with Stewart and Ann that their "wilderness experience" is over and that it ended so happily. Who knows why these difficult times happen. Some say that the Lord brings all of our trials to strengthen us, others say that Satan brings all our tribulations to defeat us, and others say that our problems occur because we live in a fallen world with sinful men. We humans are always searching for reasons why, but the truth is that all of the above probably apply part of the time and none apply all of the time, and we are not usually going to know the source of our pain. And it really doesn't matter. What's important is not what caused our situation but what we do with it. Regardless of the origin, Romans 8:28 is always operating: "In all things God works for the good of those who love him, who have been called according to his purpose." We know that God can and will use every circumstance to grow us and strengthen us and reveal His faithfulness to us if we will allow Him to do so.

Jesus said, "In this world you will have trouble" (John 16:33). Not *might* have trouble but *will* have trouble! Yes, there will be struggle, disappointment, pain and even failure. But then Jesus added, "But take heart! I have overcome the world." Jesus is always there, walking with us through everything and using our struggles to our ultimate benefit.

I'm guessing that you can identify with Stewart and Gideon because you have had trials at some point that have seemingly gone from bad to worse as well, but the resulting victory strengthened you and heightened your faith and trust in God. We can praise Him in the midst of pain because we know that "joy comes in the morning" (Ps. 30:5), and we can praise Him when the morning comes because of His faithfulness to see us through.

> Because of the LORD's great love, we are not consumed.
> > for his compassions never fail,
> They are new every morning;
> > great is your faithfulness. (Lam. 3:22–23)

6

Choosing to Praise God

IN TIMES OF LONELINESS

MAYBE I should have entitled this chapter "Praising God in Times of Aloneness." Loneliness and aloneness are closely related, but one does not necessarily trigger the other. We can be alone without being lonely, and we can be lonely even though we're not alone. What I'm talking about here is that awful state of being separated—not part of the group, different in some way. Know the feeling?

Leah did. Maybe you remember her story (Gen. 27–35). She was the older of two sisters, and she had the misfortune to be, shall we say, homely, while her younger sister Rachel was evidently drop-dead gorgeous. At least Jacob thought so.

The wheels of the story started rolling when Jacob fled his home and family because he had hoodwinked his twin brother Esau out of his birthright. Esau was understandably none too happy and threatened to kill Jacob. So Jacob fled and went to Haran, his mother's homeland. There he met Rachel and immediately fell head over heels in love with her.

So Jacob contracted with Rachel's father Laban to work for him for free for seven years; in exchange, Laban would then give him Rachel to marry. Jacob worked and prospered Laban, and after seven years the wedding took place. Imagine Jacob's excitement to be marrying the woman of his dreams, the woman he had worked for seven years to wed. Then imagine his outrage and disappointment to discover the next morning that Laban had tricked him and had given him Leah instead.

Put yourself in Leah's place. She spent her wedding night with a man who was not loving her; he thought it was Rachel in his arms. And my guess is that the next morning Jacob made no effort to cover his displeasure when he saw Leah in the daylight without her veil.

Jacob went to Laban who explained that he had given him Leah because he could not allow him to marry Rachel until her older sister was first married; it was tradition. *Maybe he could have mentioned that a little earlier?* But Jacob agreed to work for another seven years for Rachel; he married her a few days later and then fulfilled his seven-year obligation.

I can imagine that Leah was not only alone in her marriage but alone in society. Back then someone with a physical defect was often ostracized. People only wanted to associate with the lovely, the whole. She was different. She wasn't pretty. Many scholars speculate that she had an eye problem that contributed to her unattractiveness. And now she shared her husband with her beautiful, younger sister. I can think of few things worse. Jacob loved Rachel and got stuck with Leah, and Leah knew it. But she loved Jacob anyway.

So maybe you wonder, where was God in all of this? God did not forget Leah. Scripture says: "When the LORD saw that Leah was not loved, he opened her womb, but Rachel was barren. Leah became pregnant and gave birth to a son. She named him Reuben, for she said, 'It is because the Lord has seen my misery. Surely my husband will love me now'" (Gen. 29:31–33). Leah still longed to be loved.

And when she bore Simeon and then Levi, she hoped again and again that Jacob would love her because she was giving him sons. But it didn't happen.

Then when she bore her fourth son Judah, she realized that Jacob would not love her. She said, "This time I will praise the LORD " (Gen. 29:35). Wow, Leah finally got it. She knew that even if she had twenty sons, Jacob was not ever going to love her as much as he loved Rachel. Having come to that realization, she turned her affection to the One who did love her completely and unconditionally—her Lord.

God balanced the books a bit. When one area of our lives is lacking, sometimes God will give us abundance in another area to compensate. In this case Rachel had Jacob's love, but Leah had Jacob's sons.

Was Leah still lonely? Yes. Did her situation change? No. But praising God changed her. It changed her spirit, her expectations, her unrealistic dreams. She recognized that God was worthy to be trusted, and she redirected her love to Him. I suspect that her acknowledgment of God's sovereignty in her life—that He had blessed her in other ways—caused her to be more content, more at peace, more happy. I suspect that she enjoyed a closeness to God that others didn't have.

My disability is different from Leah's, yet I identify with her because we're both different because of physical appearance. And although society has come a long, long way in understanding and accepting people with disabilities, there is still that stigma, at least in the minds of some people.

Like Leah, I feel different. I can't walk or throw a ball or get myself up a step. I can't stand up and speak to someone eye-to-eye; in a crowd, I'm at eye level with everybody else's backsides. I can't wade out into the ocean or sit in a normal chair in a restaurant or theater. I want to be included in what everybody else is doing, but because of physical limitations, sometimes I simply cannot.

When I go to a football or a basketball game and the group of parents and friends I'd like to sit with is in the middle of the bleachers ten rows up, there's no way I can get up to them, so I have to be content to sit at the bottom in the handicapped seating area. And when I go to wedding receptions, I'd absolutely love to get up and dance; I loved to dance! But I must be content to sit on the sidelines and watch others hit the dance floor and spin to the music. Those are times when I feel separated.

And I so appreciate those who scramble to help me find a ramp so I can be at the top of those stairs or who push me out onto the dance floor in my motorized wheelchair and spin me around, but still, it's different. I would like to be like everybody else, but I'm not. Please know I'm not sitting on the pity pot here—just sharing a few of the ways I feel different. I'll bet you have a list too.

This brings to mind one of those occasions when I felt separated. At the end of our son Daniel's sopho-more year, we were invited to attend a banquet for his high school chamber choir (how blessed I am that the one child God gave us shares my love for music!) to be held in San Clemente at the lovely home of the parents of one of the choir members. Having dropped Daniel off at this house a few times before, I had made a men-tal note that there were no steps leading up to the front door, so I felt comfortable that I would be able to get in and out of the home with no problem, so this time I didn't call ahead like I usually do to see if I'd need to make special arrangements. Big mistake.

There was one step at the entrance that I had over-looked, but we had a short ramp in the car, so Mike put that down, and I crossed over and went into the house. Much to my dismay, we immediately saw that there were two steps up into the living room that led to the backyard. Dead end for me and my chair.

So we went back out, back down my portable ramp, and rolled to the left side of the house to the gate that led to the backyard. Mike opened the gate, and we saw that there were many steps down to the party area. Can't do that. So I rolled back out to the driveway, and Mike and I took a few minutes to problem solve. Of course, we've been in these situations before, but this one seemed particularly disappointing because the event was to award the students' talents and accomplishments and to honor the choir director who wasn't returning to the school the following year. Usually I can just brush it off, but this time I was frustrated, disappointed and, I admit, a bit angry—not at anyone but at the situation. Why hadn't I called ahead? My physical disability was causing me to be separated from the party I wanted so much to attend.

There really was no solution, so I told Mike, "You go on to the party [which was starting] and have a good time. I'll go back to the van and crank up the music or get in some good prayer time. Really, I'm fine with that." And I was. Mike objected, but I assured him that this was the best option.

Just as we started for the van, the hostess came out. "Renée, I heard you were having a hard time getting in. I've got another way that might work." She took me around to the right side of the yard and asked if I could go across the grass. I replied, "Yep, I can off-road easily," so I bounced across the grass to a spot where I could see the party area, but everybody was another level down. I could see the tops of a few people's heads, and I could see a few people standing on the top level, but I couldn't hear what was being said.

I saw that it wasn't going to work, no matter what. So I looked up to the heavens and had a brief moment with God: *God, I know there is nothing I can do to change this. So I praise You for the spectacular ocean out there in the distance, for the beautiful evening and beautiful weather and beautiful sunset that we're just starting to experience. I praise You, Lord, and now I'm heading back to the van.* And you know what? It became okay. Not getting to go to the party suddenly wasn't as important as it had been because I remembered that I have so much to be thankful for.

At that moment the hostess said, "You know, I'm kind of kicking myself. There's a woman two doors down who moved in recently who is a quadriplegic just like you. You might know her—she's one of the two joggers who was hit by a drunk driver on the Pacific Coast Highway."

"You're kidding me! Carol? She moved two doors down from you? I had suggested that she look for a house in this neighborhood because you have such beautiful views of the ocean!"

I'd met Carol five years earlier, soon after the accident that had left her quadriplegic. Her sister-in-law

Traci had come with Dana, an ex-student from San Clemente High, to decorate our house for Christmas. (A God appointment?) Two months later when the drunk driver hit Carol and another woman on PCH, I heard about it; everybody in the area heard about it. It was horrible! Soon afterward Traci called and identified herself, explained that one of the victims was Carol, her sister-in-law, and that now Carol was a quadriplegic like me, and asked if I would talk to her. Of course, I readily agreed to assist her in any way I could. But I shared with Traci that right then I was probably the last person Carol would want to see because when people are newly injured, they typically don't want to see anyone in a wheelchair. They don't want to accept that that's going to be them. They want to believe that they're going to recover. I know; I was there once. So I told Traci that when the time came, when Carol was ready, I'd be happy to talk about accessibility issues for her home and to explain to her about attendant care—how to go about hiring an attendant, how much to pay her, how to train her, etc.

A few weeks later Traci called and said, "Carol came home from the hospital. Her mother-in-law and I want to learn everything we can about her care." So I invited them to come over and watch what my caregiver does with me on a shower day and then come back the next day, which is not a shower day, so they could get the whole picture and see what the morning routine for a quadriplegic entails.

While the words were coming out of my mouth, I was thinking, *Do I really want to offer that? It's so embarrassing. They'll see parts of my body that I'm embarrassed for anyone to see.* You'd think I would have given up on modesty a long time ago, but some things you never get used to. But my heart was breaking for this family, and stronger than my modesty was my desire to help them get through this. It was a crash course in anatomy, a crash course in care giving, a crash course in hygiene, a crash course in human psychology—of how to work with the injured person and caregiver. It was simply the best way to educate them. And so they came.

At the end of the session, I told Traci, "Whenever you think Carol is ready to meet someone in a chair, let me know." When that time came, Carol and her husband Craig invited Mike and me over to their house to meet them and share some of the ins and outs of this road we didn't choose but nevertheless were both now traveling. It was the beginning of a rewarding friendship between Carol and me. I kept in touch with her, and she would call me from time to time when she had questions.

When we'd first met Carol and Craig, they lived in a two-story house in a very kid-friendly neighborhood. She did not want to uproot her children, so they stayed in that house. Problem was that Carol was confined to the downstairs. After four years, she reached the point of being willing to consider moving to a one-story home where she could have full access to her family. Fast forward to me discovering that Carol was now living two houses down from where I was sitting.

So I said, "Would you mind looking down the street to see if Carol's van is in her driveway? If it is, she's home, and maybe I can pop over to her house and visit while you guys are having the banquet." She checked and the van was there, so she walked down and talked to Carol and came back and reported that Carol was eager to have me come down.

As I rolled down to Carol's house, all my frustration and feelings of being left out evaporated, and I was excited. *Perfect!* I had wanted to go see Carol's new house but just hadn't had the opportunity, and here it was!

I rolled into the kitchen where Carol and Craig were having dinner; it hadn't occurred to me that it was dinner time. I offered to leave and not interrupt their meal, but they insisted that I stay, so we enjoyed a good visit while they ate. After dinner Craig went to see about something else, so it was just Carol and me and her thirteen-year-old daughter Claire. I got the tour of the house and was so excited to see how beautiful it was and how accessible it was for Carol. I was so happy for her that now she could get into her kids' rooms and be together again with her husband. I enjoyed getting to know Claire, and the three of us sat and talked for maybe an hour and a half. The banquet and earlier frustration were far from my mind.

Then Mike, Daniel and his friend Ted came to pick me up. It was really sweet to see Daniel interact with

Carol—he smiled big and gave her a hug. Then he shook Craig's hand. And I was especially touched by how comfortable and warm Ted was with them; just like Daniel, he offered a hug and a handshake. I had a moment: *Wow, God. How great that You've used my wheelchair to help my son be comfortable around people who have disabilities—and it's even rubbed off on Ted!*

Looking back on the evening, I was shocked that I was able to change my attitude so quickly. In the past that wasn't always the case. But after some thought I realized the turning point was when I remembered to praise God for His amazing creation. My situation didn't change, but my attitude sure did. No, I didn't get to go to the party, but God replaced it with something even better.

Leah got something better too. God gave her six sons and a daughter plus two more sons by her maidservant. These eight sons became eight of the twelve tribes of Israel. That's two thirds! But the highest honor for Leah is that Jesus came from the line of her fourth son Judah—not Rachel's well-known and great son Joseph, but Judah, the one who made Leah realize that her love would come from God. What a blessing! God did not forget Leah but blessed her in ways she could not have imagined.

For many years Rachel did not have children. She finally bore Joseph, and then she died young while giving birth to her second son Benjamin. Jacob buried her near Bethlehem on his trip back to his homeland (Gen. 35:19).

Scripture says that many years later, just before Jacob died, he gave instructions that he wished to be buried in the family plot. "There they buried Abraham and Sarah his wife. There they buried Isaac and Rebekah his wife, and there I buried Leah" (Gen. 49:31). It's sweet that Jacob says, "I buried Leah." He made a point of saying that Leah too was in the family cemetery and that he personally buried her there. It seems very respectful. I like to think that in later years Jacob came to recognize Leah's inner beauty and felt some kind of love and appreciation for her.

Obviously, my disappointment at not getting to attend one party on one evening completely pales in comparison to the years Leah suffered feelings of rejection and loneliness. However, I submit that the same principle applies. In the same way that my taking a few minutes to offer praise to God lifted my spirit and changed my outlook, paving the way for me to enjoy the rest of the evening, I believe, albeit on a much grander scale, that Leah's acceptance of God's love for her changed her outlook and paved the way to a fulfilling life for her. Leah could have become bitter, resentful and jealous. Instead, she opened herself up to God's blessings. She wasn't the favorite wife, but God replaced that hole in her heart with the love of her nine children and, more importantly, His love for her. She wasn't alone or lonely because she welcomed God's presence with her. The same was true of me. The same can be true of you.

7

Choosing to Praise God

IN TIMES OF GREAT LOSS

YOU may have heard it said that exercising our faith is like sitting on a chair. It's a lovely chair, sturdy by all appearances. Others have sat in the chair and told exciting stories of how it held them up, so you have reason to think the chair will probably hold you. However, the only way to know for sure is to sit on it yourself. But sometimes we look at the chair and say, "I don't want to sit there." But God gently pulls us to that place because His plans are bigger than ours—often different but always perfect.

I am eager for you to meet my friend Jana Alayra. Or perhaps you know her already. Jana is a singer/ songwriter who performs her upbeat children's songs in churches and conferences nationwide. She has a God-given talent for putting Scripture to music and adding hand and body movements, which results in millions of children singing God's word, jumping up and down and moving their hands right along with her, whether in an auditorium or in their family rooms watching one of her DVDs. In addition, Jana has a ministry to adults, especially women, and she shares her powerful testimony and message of hope to audiences across the United States.

Jana has sat in a chair she would never have imagined or chosen, and she learned for herself that God really is sufficient to hold her up. She's here to share her story of loss and hope with you.

> When I put my four-year-old daughter Lynnie down for her nap that afternoon, I could not have known that it would be the last time I'd kiss those precious, chubby cheeks.
>
> May 26, 1996, started out like any ordinary day. That morning Lynnie, my older daughter Haley and I enjoyed skating around the neighborhood. We had a lot of fun laughing and enjoying the southern California weather on that Memorial Day weekend. About 4:30 p.m. I left with the kids, including my one-year-old daughter Brittany and a babysitter, to go to Saddleback Church in Lake Forest (where Rick Warren is pastor), because I was scheduled to sing at their evening service.
>
> Heading south toward the church, I exited the freeway, and that's when it happened. I didn't see the red light. A pickup broadsided my Mazda MPV. I was aware of crashing noises, flying glass, crying and screaming, and being jerked and slammed around. Injured and somewhat disoriented, I turned to check on the children. Haley and

Brittany were both crying. And then I looked at Lynnie and saw her eyes. I knew she was gone. I could see that she was no longer there. I was thrown into what most moms would say is their worst nightmare.

A bystander put her arms around me and led me over to the curb. Lynnie's lifeless little body was now on the pavement in the middle of the intersection. A tangle of firefighters and paramedics hovered over her and worked on her. I had cracked a couple of ribs, so I sat on the curb trying to catch my breath and I prayed; I desperately begged God to bring Lynnie back. *Jesus, please let her live. Please let her live. Please let her live!* As I prayed, I experienced a supernatural moment in which I realized that, even though my little Lynnie was only twenty-five yards away, I could not reach her. She was out of my hands, and her life was out of my control. I felt myself letting go. I believe that the Lord Himself was there, reminding me that although I was powerless, He was in control of the situation and of Lynnie's eternal life. It struck me like a sword piercing to the deepest part of my soul that I had to let go and had to trust God to be who I knew Him to be.

I recall silently reasoning with Him: *Oh, God! You better be who You've promised to be. Jesus better be real. Eternal life better be real, because, if not, I won't be able to survive this.* I realized that He was my only hope and my only strength at this horrible moment and in all those moments that would follow the loss of my precious Lynnie. It seemed like I could feel my heavenly Father looking right into my eyes, right into my soul, and He was asking, "Do you trust Me, Jana?" What could I do? I had long ago fallen in love with my Savior and Lord. For over twenty years I had read His Word and clung to His words of hope and eternal life. This was an all or nothing proposition—

either I trusted Him or I didn't, and if I didn't, there was nothing left but despair. So on that curb I could only let go and say with all that's in me, *I trust You. She is Yours.*

The woman beside me began praying softly, "Lord, You are faithful. You know this woman's life. Protect her and comfort her. You will be her future; You will be her peace." I felt God's peace. God sent that woman to tell me what was true—that God was with me and would help me through this.

What happened after this defies description. It was like I was enveloped in a cloud that I could almost feel, a cloud of peace, of quiet, and of almighty God's power and love. I could almost hear Him saying, "Keep trusting Me, Jana. Keep trusting Me. I am God. I do keep My promises. My Son is the source of eternal life. Fear not and keep trusting Me. Keep your eyes on Me!"

Afterward I struggled with unbearable regret. If only I'd seen that red light. If only I'd left at a different time. If only I'd taken a different route. But I began to realize that I could not go there, that these thoughts were the words of the enemy. I knew self-incriminations would destroy me if I let them. At least I could be thankful that no one else in my van was seriously injured and that the occupants of the pickup truck were not hurt.

In the weeks and months immediately following the accident, I had some of the most powerful and sweet encounters with my Lord that I will probably ever experience. A couple of times I woke out of a deep sleep with my hands lifted in the air, reaching for Him, reaching for my Lord out of complete childlike dependence. Because I knew my strength came from Him, I felt utterly powerless without Him. I was filled with a new clarity about the reality of God and of heaven, and I was thankful, so very thankful.

The first time I went to visit Lynnie's grave was before the marker was placed there. I remembered exactly
where the grave was—on a quiet hill in a beautiful me-
morial park overlooking the Pacific Ocean. I sprawled
out face down in the new grass covering Lynnie's grave
and sobbed. But in the middle of that sobbing, I was
inexplicably worshiping. I was weeping both out of the
sorrow of missing Lynnie and out of joy and gratitude
that she wasn't under that dirt or in that coffin. Because
of Jesus, she wasn't in that grave. She was alive! And I
praised Jesus and thanked Him. I knew that Lynnie was
in heaven, and I could imagine her there with her chub-
by cheeks sitting on Jesus' lap. I was overtaken by how
thankful I was—for the gift of eternal life, for Jesus, for
His generosity.

It all made so much more sense to me. I knew that
Jesus long ago saw my suffering (and everyone else's) and
that He died to defeat death and remove its sting. *Praise
You, Jesus!* I sat up and sang songs of praise right there,
right there on my Lynnie's grave. Never could I have
imagined it would be possible that on the grave of my
daughter I could sing songs of praise and worship to my
Lord with a grateful heart. What a powerful surprise that
was and continues to be in my life!

The faith I sing about is even more real because part
of me is already in heaven. I emerged from this experience with a stronger sense of my faith and with a new
mission to reach out to children and adults. I feel especially compelled to bring solace to those who have had a
similar experience. If I can bring the blessing of comfort
to someone who is grieving, I consider it a unique privilege.

Sometimes I think of Mary, the mother of Jesus.
I'm struck by the words recorded in Scripture: "Mary

treasured up all these things and pondered them in her heart" (Luke 2:19). These words speak to me in a powerful way. No one could understand what was going on in her heart—the joy, the fear, the thrill, the powerful touch of the Holy Spirit upon her. It was just between her and God. There have been many times when I have had a similar deep, abiding, powerful sense of peace and trust in the Lord because of this horrific loss. Sometimes I think people might think I'm a little crazy to feel that way. But His peace is real. I'm not delusional, stifled or in denial. I know as firmly as the ground I stand on that I have a daughter who was scooped up into heaven where her faith has become sight. She sees things I long to see— namely, Jesus. One day I will see Him too!

To a lesser extent but by the same power of the Holy Spirit, I, like Mary, treasure these things and ponder them in my heart. I don't think I can ever explain it adequately. I trust My Lord. I love Him even more after having to let go of something so precious. I see Him working. I know one day when I see Lynnie again in heaven, we will rejoice and praise God for how He worked through this trial to do unimaginable and eternally priceless things. For now, I trust Him, and I treasure these things.

After reading Jana's account, are you as moved as I am? Is that not one of the most touching stories you've ever heard? Bearing the grief of the death of a child is a chair no mother wants to sit in. But in sitting in that chair, Jana experienced a closeness to God that otherwise would have been impossible, and she learned that God is who He says He is and that He will do what He says He will do. Jana now knows what she previously thought—God is faithful and sufficient, even in our darkest valley.

In the now-famous poem "Footprints" by Mary Stevenson, a man dreams that he's walking on the beach with the Lord and sees two sets of footprints in the sand—one set his and one set God's. But he notices that in the lowest and saddest times of his life, there's only one set. So the man asked God why He abandoned him when he needed Him most. God replied, "My son, my precious child. I love you and would never leave you. During your times of trial and suffering when you see only one set of footprints, it was then that I carried you." In the same way, God carried Jana through this horrendous tragedy, and He's eager to do the same for you and me.

Did you notice Jana's surprising response? She put her trust in God, and she actually *praised* Him. She praised Him for being in control. She praised Him for His comfort and peace. She praised Him for dying to give Lynnie life in heaven, and she praised Him that she would some day see Lynnie again and see Jesus face to face.

For any of you who might be a bit skeptical that this was truly an honest response, let me assure you that it's true. Spending time with Jana—whether it's on stage, at lunch or ministering together in a women's prison—I see the peace in her eyes. This peace is not humanly possible given her loss but can only come from the Holy Spirit.

I'm reminded of the story of King David when he

and Bathsheba lost their son. The child was taken ill, so David fasted and prayed and lay on the ground; he was so intent on begging God to spare the lad's life that no one could move him. During that time his servants were afraid of him, and when the child died on the seventh day, they hesitated to give David the news for fear that he would do something destructive. Such is the anguish of a parent when facing the reality that his/her child might be taken.

The boy did die, but David didn't react as expected. When he learned that the boy was dead, he arose, bathed, put on clean clothes and went into the house of the Lord to worship. To worship! And then he ate and drank, and when the servants inquired as to his actions, he said, "I will go to him, but he will not return to me" (2 Sam. 12:23). David had the assurance that he would see his son again in heaven.

The conditions surrounding the death of David's son and the accident that took Jana's daughter are vastly different, but I would like for you to notice some similarities. First, both Jana and King David praised the Lord. They worshiped. Second, their pain was great, but they had the assurance that they would see their children in heaven. What a blessed promise!

One of my favorite Scriptures is First Thessalonians 5:18: "In everything give thanks; for this is God's will for you" (NASB). Jana certainly wasn't thankful that Lynnie was dead, but she was thankful for the way the Lord prepared her and comforted her, and she was thankful that her daughter was safe in heaven in the arms of Jesus. She and King David were thankful that they would see their children again. Please know that I don't say these next words flippantly: even in our worst disaster we can find reasons to be thankful if we look for them instead of being solely focused on the tragedy. When we submit to God and praise Him, He can bless us and comfort us, just like He did for Jana, just like He did for David.

Even in times of great loss, let us remember Psalm 18:1–2:

> I love you, O LORD, my strength.
> The LORD is my rock, my fortress and my deliverer;
> my God is my rock, in whom I take refuge.
> He is my shield and the horn of my salvation, my stronghold.

8

Choosing to Praise God

WHEN YOU ARE AFRAID

THE word "fear" covers a myriad of situations. We're afraid we're going to look foolish. We're afraid of being left out or not being accepted. We're afraid of having an accident. We're afraid of losing a loved one. We're afraid of failing. We're afraid of rejection. We're afraid of contracting a disease. We're afraid of spiders and bugs and snakes. We're afraid of the dark.

I don't pretend to know the mind of God, but I can speculate that God equipped us with the fear trigger for our own protection; our fear warns us of legitimate impending danger and gives us the opportunity to take action or get to safety. However, sometimes it irrationally flips into gear.

Whether our fear is legitimate or irrational, it can grow like yeast in dough, consuming us until we're totally panicked. In times like these, we can forget that we serve the God of the universe who is in control and who will give us peace if we ask!

When I think of fear in my life, I remember the time when Sacred Heart Catholic Church in Saratoga, California, invited me to give a concert to kick off their annual concert series. One of the many ministries of this church is an outreach program to the men at San Quentin Prison, so in addition to the concert, the producer/coordinator asked me to go to San Quentin and give a program for the inmates.

Although I was a bit anxious about going to the granddaddy of all prisons where the meanest of the mean were incarcerated, I didn't think too much about it, because about six months prior to this, I had given a similar concert at the Downey Youth Authority, where my good friend, Father Leo Celano, was the chaplain. Those twelve to eighteen-year-old felons filed into the room in a very rigid, orderly fashion and were not allowed to come closer to me than ten feet. There were armed guards leaning against the walls all around the large hall. I assumed the security at San Quentin would be at least that tight.

With looking after a toddler, having company visiting, and Mike's busy work schedule, I was distracted and hadn't thought to mention the San Quentin appearance to him until we were on the airplane flying up to San Francisco. When I remembered, I said, "Oh, by the way, tomorrow afternoon they want us to go up to San Quentin." Mike just looked at me. There are very few things that he clamps down on, but he said, "What?! No! I'm not comfortable letting you go to San Quentin." The protector in him emerged.

I laughed and said, "Really?" But he repeated, this time even more emphatically, "No! How can I defend you if something goes wrong?" The look on his face showed deep concern and fear for my safety. It was my job when we arrived to tell my concert coordinator how strongly Mike felt. There was much discussion, but the end result was that the San Quentin outreach was too far into the plans to be cancelled. Once he heard the inevitable, Mike was not happy with me. I felt horrible, and he dragged his heels all the way there. I vowed to be more thoughtful to fill him in on future travel details.

The next day we pulled up to the prison—big walls topped with razor wire, a tall watchtower that looked out over the San Francisco Bay. Pretty daunting. We checked in and were escorted into a room; the door slammed behind us. We passed through that room and into another area that looked like a cage with bars floor to ceiling, and again the gate slammed behind us. We went through three of these caged areas, and every time I could sense Mike getting more and more uptight. To diffuse the tension, I tried to make light of it all, but Mike was not in good humor, and I felt badly that I had put him in that position.

Finally we arrived at the big hall where the concert was to take place. The stage had no steps up to it, which meant I had to be lifted up. I could see and feel that with every move, Mike was getting more and more nervous.

Four big guys dressed in their blue inmate jumpsuits came in unsupervised; the jumpsuits were the only tip-off that they were residents there. They moved to the base of the stage and started setting up equipment—drums, keyboard, bass and guitar. Then they started jamming, and I quickly realized that they were good—really good! The players saw our dilemma and offered to help. They lifted me up on stage, and I proceeded with my sound check. When finished, I remained on the platform but rolled back into the corner, waiting for my cue to begin my program.

The inmates who would be the audience for my testimony/concert had earned the privilege to attend. They started filtering into the room, about two hundred of them casually strolling in through several doors. With admitted alarm, I couldn't help but notice that, unlike my previous experience, there were no guards! *No guards? No guns? Hmm. I wonder what Mike is thinking.*

Then the service began. The worship band started playing, and a twenty-voice choir of inmates came up on stage and sang a choral number and then broke into praise and worship, clapping and swaying to the music. It was rowdy and loud. And there I sat on the corner of the stage taking it all in and getting a tad nervous. With time on my hands, my imagination started to kick in.

I started thinking of movies in which prisoners intentionally made a lot of noise to distract or cover up a covert plan to escape or to injure someone. These guys were outrageously good musicians, and they sounded great, so I should have been enjoying their beautiful worship, but I confess that I was intimidated by what I imagined had given them a ticket to San Quentin, and I was uneasy. Actually a bit scared.

Then it was my turn. As I was being introduced, the warden came over to me, bent down and whispered in my ear, "Renée, see that little camera in the way back of the room?"

"Yes."

"That's for our boys who are on death row. Would you mind saying a few words to them during the concert?"

What?!

"Welcome, Renée Bondi!" The music started, and I was on. That was it. No more time to think about it. I'm sure I had the look of a deer in the headlights! I rolled out singing my first song, "Be Not Afraid": "Be not afraid. I go before you always. Come, follow Me, and I will give you rest." And as I was singing, a big chill came down my neck as a scene from the movie *Dead Man Walking* flashed across my mind. I froze. The picture in my mind was from the very end of the movie when a nun (played by Susan Sarandon) sat with the inmate (Sean Penn) as he awaited execution. She sang to him, and the song she sang was "Be not afraid. I go before you always. Come, follow Me, and I will give you rest." So there I was, looking into that little camera, singing the same song to those men whose lives were scheduled to end the same way. *Have any of them seen the movie? Ugh. Out of all the songs I could have sung tonight . . .* I thought. Coincidence? Or God speaking to and touching the men?

During my presentation I addressed the men on death row, saying, "For all of you here, but especially for those watching from their cells, I want to say that I am in my own form of prison—a body that doesn't let me do things the way I'd like. But the more I lean on God and surrender my life, my pain and fear to Him, the more I'm reminded that heaven exists and that we will all be set free one day. But the key is surrendering our lives to Him."

I completed the concert and testimony, and the men were very attentive and responsive. Then it was question and answer time. Now remember, I was on stage, the unguarded inmates in the front row were no more than ten feet away, and Mike was way in the back at the sound board. The first question came from a man in the back. He stood up and asked, "What was your emotion when you first found out you were pregnant?"

I thought, *What an interesting question coming from a male San Quentin inmate!* Caught off guard by the fact that such an intimate question would come from such a hardcore-looking guy, I replied, "I had the feeling that I was at the top of the roller coaster just before I plummeted down the track. We're on this ride, and here we go! I remember praying, 'Lord, I don't know how I'm going to raise a child from a wheelchair without the use of my hands and feet. Please be with us every step of the way.'"

I fielded more commonly asked questions, and we were winding down, so I said, "Okay, we have time for one more." A man in the front row stood and said, "Ma'am, I think it's pretty wonderful what God has done in your life and how you've been able to turn your life around. And we are very thankful that you've come, ma'am. But I think the person that all us men here really want to meet is your husband. Is he here?"

I started giggling. For a moment I thought about not introducing him because I knew how uncomfortable he was, but I quickly realized I couldn't do that. So I flashed an apologetic smile to Mike and gestured to the back of the room, responding, "As a matter of fact, *he is!*" Mike reluctantly pushed his chair back and slowly rose to his feet while all two hundred men stood up, turned around and gave him a standing ovation.

I sat there in awe, shaking my head, and whispered, "Wow, God. Wow."

Now it was time to leave. I assumed everybody would file out and would need to return quickly to their cells. I couldn't get off the stage until someone lifted me up and off, so I rolled back to the corner of the stage, indicating I was no longer "on." But as I did, about ten of the inmates stepped up on the stage and started walking toward me. I was smiling on the outside, but on the inside I was freaking out! You see, when you have absolutely no way to protect yourself—no ability to run or hit or kick an assailant, you feel even more vulnerable and exposed to danger. Mike was in the back, so he couldn't see me or I him. In that moment I started praying, *Okay, God, You're going to honor what we just did here, right? You're going to shield me, right? This was of You, right? Please Lord, protect me!* I know, a pretty pushy prayer, but I was starting to panic.

When the first guy reached me, he knelt down and looked up with the kindest eyes and said, "I want to thank you," and he started to share his story that he was a white-collar crime guy from Laguna Niguel. Then another guy came up, and another—all basically to give me a hug and say thank you. Any one of these guys could have been my neighbors at home, and they were very appreciative that they had not been forgotten, that Mike and I had taken the time to come be with them.

And so it ended. I had sung and spoken at San Quentin. I went in hopes that my story and music would touch these men, but when it was over, I knew that it was I who had been touched.

On the way home, I was reliving the evening. I said to Mike, "It was an amazing experience—so incredible, a real eye-opener. How did you feel about it?"

Mike laughed and replied, "We're never doing this again!"

But we have, many times. Mike would tell you that prison ministry has come to hold a very special place in our hearts. That day Matthew 25:36 came alive: "I was in prison and you came to visit me." I realized that I feel drawn to working with the incarcerated. As I was speaking and singing at the youth authority, I gazed into the eyes of those kids. I remember looking into the eyes of one guy whose eyes were stark, cold as ice, like he had a huge wall up. And then my eyes would shift to the guy next to him, and he'd have eyes like a hungry puppy dog, saying *I want to know more! Tell me everything!* And then my eyes would roam to the next guy who was like the first: *I'm tough. Don't you dare think you can soften me with that wheelchair.* And then maybe the fourth might be young and impressionable, also eager to hear, like he was hoping someone could give him something positive to help him out of his present situation. I could see it all in their eyes, because the eyes really are the windows to the soul. These boys and all men and women who are imprisoned are people with real feelings and disappointments and hurts and hopes. God loves them as much as He loves me, and they need Him as much as I do.

Fear is a funny thing. And how we respond to it can change outcomes. Looking back, our fear was very real, but as it turned out, a bit unwarranted. As you probably noticed, we let our imaginations run wild before turning to God. Fear can be a rational response to a situation, but when it paralyzes or prevents us from taking appropriate action, it must be put into check.

I'm reminded of Jehoshaphat, the king of Judah, who had good reason to be afraid (2 Chron. 20). The kings of Moab, Ammon and Mount Seir declared war on Judah, and word reached Jehoshaphat that a vast army was marching against his country. The king was badly shaken at the news because he had a very small army. But knowing God's sovereignty and power, he went straight to the Lord. He then announced that all the people of Judah would fast and pray for a season in penitence and intercession.

The citizens converged on Jerusalem, and Jehoshaphat stood among them and prayed:

> Oh LORD God of our fathers, are you not the God who is in heavens? You rule over all the kingdoms of the nations. Power and might are in your hand, and no one can withstand you. O our God, did you not drive out the inhabitants of this land before your people Israel and give it forever to the descendants of Abraham your friend? They have lived in it and have built in it a sanctuary for your Name, saying, "If calamity comes upon us, whether the sword of judgment, or plague or famine, we will stand in your presence before this temple that bears your Name and will cry out to you in our distress, and you will hear us and save us." (20:6–9)

This passage is all about praise. No, the word isn't there, but notice how Jehoshaphat remembers the mighty works God has done and gives Him credit. He acknowledges that God is powerful and mighty, that He gave them the land and that they know that they can depend on Him in such a time as this. Pure praise. It's not about saying the word; it's about telling God you know who He is and what He's done through the ages and that you honor, revere and trust Him!

Then a prophet of the Lord told Jehoshaphat and all the people, "Don't be afraid or discouraged because of this vast army. For the battle is not yours but God's" (20:15). At that point the king and all the people fell down and worshiped the Lord. The next morning Judah's little army marched out, and Jehoshaphat stopped and called them to attention: "Have faith in the LORD your God and you will be upheld; have faith in his prophets and you will be successful" (20:20). Then he called out a choir who led the march singing, "Give thanks to the LORD, for his love endures forever" (20:21). They praised and thanked the Lord as they marched along and sang of His greatness.

And what happened to the armies that were attacking Judah is incredible. At the very moment that the choir began to praise and thank God, the Lord caused the invading armies to turn on each other. First, Moab and Ammon ganged up on Mount Seir and killed every soldier. Then Moab and Ammon turned on each other, and not a soldier was left alive! When Jehoshaphat and his army arrived, as far as they could see, there were dead bodies on the ground. It took his army three days to gather all the plunder.

Take a wild guess what they did next—they praised the Lord! With Jehoshaphat leading the way and accompanied by a band of harps, lyres and trumpets, they marched into Jerusalem and into the Temple, praising God for the amazing rescue. I bet that was a spectacular sight to see!

I've learned a few truths from this story. When faced with almost sure annihilation, Jehoshaphat's first reaction was to go to the Lord. During the crisis they praised God and trusted Him to protect them, and after God delivered them, they remembered to give Him credit. I think we can safely assume that God gave us this story so that we would know that what was true for Jehoshaphat is true for us—the battle is not ours but the Lord's.

"Be not afraid. I go before you always. Come, follow Me, and I will give you rest."

9

Choosing to Praise God

WHEN THINGS LOOK HOPELESS

WINSTON CHURCHILL was once invited to give the graduation address at a prestigious university. When it came time for him to speak, he stood up, walked to the microphone, and said, "Never give up." He paused for several seconds and then repeated, "Never give up." Silence as everyone waited during an even longer pause. Finally, he continued. "Never, never, never, never give up!" And with that, he sat down.

How many times have you heard someone say, "I give up"? How many times have you yourself said, or felt like saying, "I give up"? When things look hopeless, why press on? It's easier and makes more sense just to quit, right?

Well, humanly speaking, that may be true. However, for those who believe in Christ, we always have hope because we have an all-powerful, all-knowing God who is able to do all things and who has promised to take care of us! In Romans 15:13 Paul writes, "May the God of hope fill you with all joy and peace as you trust in him, so that you may overflow with hope by the power of the Holy Spirit."

Paul and Silas certainly could have been discouraged in the account found in Acts 16:16–36. They delivered a fortune-telling slave girl from demonic possession, which angered her owners who were making money from her predictions. The unhappy owners hauled Paul and Silas to court. Even though Paul and Silas had broken no laws, they were stripped and beaten and thrown into the innermost dungeons of the prison where the most dangerous prisoners were held. Furthermore, they were put in stocks to ensure they would not escape.

The situation looked pretty hopeless. But Scripture says that Paul and Silas weren't thinking about the hopelessness of their circumstances, for they knew that their God was able to change their situation. Contrary to what one might expect, around midnight they were singing hymns and praising God, and the other prisoners were listening. Were they thanking God for the beatings they had received? Probably not. Were they praising Him because they enjoyed being in stocks? I seriously doubt it. Remember, Paul and Silas were sold out for Christ. I believe they realized they needed to take their focus off their physical pain and place it on the

Great Sustainer. At some point they chose to start praising God because they loved Him, because He is worthy of our praise regardless of our circumstances, because they had much to be thankful for that had nothing to do with their current situation. So impressive to me!

As they were singing praises to God, there was a great earthquake that shook the foundation of the prison, loosened their chains and opened all the doors. I think their praises had something to do with that perfectly timed earthquake. The jailer awoke from his sleep and, seeing the doors open, assumed the prisoners had fled. Knowing he'd be executed if they escaped on his watch, he drew his sword and was about to kill himself when Paul shouted, "Don't harm yourself! We are all here!" (Acts 16:28) The prisoners didn't leave when they had the chance—evidently because they knew it would mean the jailer's life. They stayed to protect him and, I suspect, to tell him about Jesus. Instantly, the jailer knew that these men had something special, so he ran to them and asked, "What must I do to be saved?" (16:30)

They replied, "Believe in the Lord Jesus, and you will be saved" (16:31). The jailer believed and so did his whole household; they were baptized and rejoiced because they believed! The jailer brought them to his house and fed them. Not only that, but when the magistrates learned that Paul and Silas were Romans (which meant they had been beaten unlawfully), they not only released them but actually begged them to leave the prison.

Wow. And I say it again—WOW! It seems that when we start praising God, He gets busy on our behalf. And it also seems that no situation is hopeless when we fully trust in God!

But not every circumstance will turn out how we want it to. Like the saying goes, "God is God, and I'm not!" At all times we must trust that God, in His divine wisdom, has a bigger, better plan than we do.

I once heard a preacher on the radio tell a great story. (I wish I could remember who he was so I could give him credit.) His son was diagnosed with cancer, so he immediately went into a time of fasting and praying for his son to be healed. For several days he fasted and prayed and didn't tell anyone. One evening the pastor was sitting in his office praying, and he reached the point at which he recognized that whether his son was healed of cancer on earth or whether he died, he was still going to be okay. Either he'd be healthy on earth or even healthier in heaven! When the preacher reached the point of being willing to accept whatever outcome the Lord had planned, he knew the fast was over. Then he realized, "I'm really hungry. I need to eat."

At that moment, someone knocked on the door to his office. When the pastor opened it, he saw one of the older ladies in his congregation standing there with a small brown bag. "Pastor," she said, "I know this sounds crazy, but the Lord told me that you need something for lunch. All I had that I could fix quick was some ham, so here's a ham sandwich."

"It was the best sandwich I ever ate," the pastor commented. He had relinquished his son to the Lord, trusting the outcome to God, and the Lord comforted him with peace . . . and a ham sandwich.

Nanette Osborn's situation reinforces God's sovereignty. Here's her story in her own words:

In 1997, I was sixty-three and working in the records office at our local hospital, supporting myself after a recent divorce. I had my routine mammogram, being conscientious to keep up my health care. A few days later, my gynecologist walked into our office, which was nothing unusual; doctors were frequently in and out of the office. Soon my boss called me over and said, "Nan, Dr. Nelson would like to speak with you." I went in and sat down with him, and like a bolt out of the blue, he said, "Nan, you have breast cancer. It showed up in your mammogram. I wanted to come over and tell you myself. I am so sorry. I'm not an oncologist so I won't be treating you, but let's talk about it."

But I couldn't talk to him. It was so totally unexpected that I was in shock. I went out to the parking lot and just stood there. I looked around and prayed, *God, where are You? I need You!*

When I returned to my desk, my boss, who knew the reason Dr. Nelson wanted to speak to me, came over and said, "Nan, I think you need to go home and call your kids."

It took me a while to be emotionally strong enough to call my daughter. Because I was so distraught, she offered to make the call to my son. In those early hours and days, I searched and begged God to be with me, while wondering if the cancer was my punishment for a second divorce. At times like this, a person's mind goes a little berserk. I had a dynamic relationship with the Lord, but for a short time I was so panicked that I wasn't thinking clearly. Then my mind cleared, and I began to remember all the ways that God had been faithful to me. *Whatever this is, I can get through it with Your help*, I told Him. *You've never left me, and I'm not leaving You!*

I went through surgery followed by the hardest chemo cocktails you could get at that time—five infusions three weeks apart, each one making me quite ill. After the chemo, I underwent six weeks of radiation, five days a week, and I sailed through that. I was a little fatigued, but because I'm part Cherokee, my skin is darker, so I didn't get the burns many fair-complexioned people get, but I did have a beautiful suntan on my left side for about six months. When I finished the treatments, the doctors told me I was cured and that the cancer would never come back.

I continued to do the Lord's work and to draw closer and closer to Him. My church family had rallied around me during the treatments, and I loved them so very much. I eagerly returned to being active in ministry but then tragedy hit—my church family got a divorce. Half the church split from the other half. I was devastated; my "family" was separated. This disappointment, combined with my second divorce and then cancer, led to depression. I prayed about what to do. A dear friend encouraged me to move near her in Oregon. I had no intention of doing that, but when I was there on a visit, God led me to a house that was perfect for me, so I bought it. I'm certain it was God's plan, for I became a part of a loving, wonderful church. The pastor gave sermons that seemed to be aimed right at me, which brought me closer still to God. I saw God again taking care of me, and I praised Him for even more evidence of His love and grace.

For many years, everything went well. But then my left arm started to hurt. I had been doing water aerobics and putting a lot of pressure on that arm, so I assumed I had pulled something. After three doctors couldn't find the problem, I went to an orthopedist who sent me for an MRI. I returned to his office for the results, ready to hear what they were going to do for this torn muscle.

The doctor's first words to me were, "Nan, do you have children?" I knew then that the problem wasn't what I was expecting. He told me I had cancer in my arm. When breast cancer travels, it usually goes to the closest appendage—in my case, my left arm. The doctor wanted me to go to Sacramento to the UC Davis Cancer Center. He knew my daughter lived near there and felt Davis would be the best place for me. He told me to go right away, not to wait, so I knew it was urgent.

A few weeks later I was at UC Davis. I went through bone scans, a nuclear exam that shows cancer, and other tests. The tests revealed that I had stage four bone cancer. On the nuclear scan, the places where the cancer existed lit up like a Christmas tree! It was all over my skull, in my neck, down my spine, in my arms (the bone in my left arm was very compromised), down to the tops of my legs—in short, my entire trunk and head were filled with cancer. Amazing that I had stage four cancer in my body and had no idea because I had no pain other than in my left arm!

My first reaction was that my arrival in heaven would be imminent. I returned to Oregon just long enough to put my house on the market, then came back to be near the hospital where they would start treatments. I didn't want to go back to the chemo that I had done before; it seemed like a last ditch effort with doubtful results, so I went on a trial system. I was happy to do it because I was eager to be involved in research that might help other cancer patients. I went in every quarter for the battery of tests, and the cancer didn't spread for three years. However, the tests then showed progression of the cancer, so the doctors put me on different meds—one to strengthen my bones plus another experimental drug.

It's hard for me to describe the peace that I've had through all of this; it's definitely from the Lord. I have had no fear, which is not characteristic of me. I know that God is surrounding me with His love and comfort. I don't dwell on the future but enjoy today. I appreciate that doctors do their part, but I know it's the Lord who is in control. And how I praise Him that I'm pain free! The doctors can't figure that one out!

One day as I was waiting for an x-ray, a young man came in with a file, looked at me, and said, "I'll be right back. I've got the wrong chart."

"Whose name is on it?" I asked.

"Nanette Osborn," he replied.

"That's me," I told him. "I'm Nan Osborn."

"No," he said. "That's not possible. What I'm reading on this chart and what I'm seeing in front of me do not match. You don't even look sick!"

I said, "Well, that's me. I have a God who loves me."

He put his hand on my shoulder and asked, "Are you a Christian?"

"Most definitely."

Then he said, "I'd like to pray for you." We prayed; then he took my x-ray and gave me a hug. It was a sweet experience.

One other time a nurse leaned over and whispered, "I want you to know I'm a Christian, too. I can't talk about it here, but I wanted you to know." I pray that the medical people will see the reason I can face this illness with hope is that I know that when the cancer completes its mission, I will cease to live on earth but will merely transfer my citizenship to heaven. My last appointment revealed spots on my liver, but the doctors and the meds aren't numbering my days; God is!

Humanly speaking, outside of a miracle from God, it looks like hope is lost for my longtime survival on this earth. But when you hold onto the Lord, hope gets better! As the saying goes, "I don't know what the future holds, but I know who holds the future." I can't wait to see the brilliant colors, the streets of gold, and the people I love who are waiting there in heaven for me.

And I know that the best is yet to come because I know that my Jesus will be there when I enter heaven. A preacher recently said, "When we get to heaven, Jesus is going to meet us with a hug." I got chills thinking about what that will be like—for Jesus to wrap His arms around me and say, "Welcome home!" Nothing could be better than that!

I praise God for the peace that He has given me. I praise Him for the fact that I have no pain; that is a miracle! I praise Him that I've outlived everybody's expectations. I praise Him that with Him, hope is never lost. Because our hope is in the one, true living God, we know that our future, whether on earth or in heaven, is secure in Him.

Wow. I pray I can have the same praise-filled attitude when my time comes to face death. Listening to Nannette share this story, I think of Psalm 31:23–24:

The LORD preserves the faithful

. . . .

Be strong and take heart,
all you who hope in the LORD.

Facing our mortality, our heart is often weakened with fear and anxiety. Remember Paul said, "For to me, to live is Christ and to die is gain" (Phil. 1:21). That's why he and Silas could praise God even in their distress; they trusted that whatever happened, they were in the care of God. We too can trust God with our life and with our death.

I find it interesting that in society we prepare so well for birth (prenatal classes, showers), we prepare so well for graduation, for marriage, for the various seasons of our life—but we do a very poor job of preparing for death, emotionally and spiritually. There's not a lot of emphasis on dying. It's a subject most prefer to avoid, but there's not one human who is going to avoid the passage from life that Nannette is now facing.

Yes, death is final. But it is only final on this earth. When we put our trust in our Lord, in our Savior, we have the hope of time without end and seeing our loved ones once again. He is saving us from death and has prepared an amazing place of beauty, peace and happiness for us after we pass from earthy life to eternity. When you find yourself facing the inevitable, it is my hope and prayer that you will be able to face it with as much peace and excitement as Nannette.

As I write this, I am bowing my head and praying for you, dear reader, that you would bow your head at this time, and ask Jesus to be Lord of your heart so that you and I can meet and dance together in heaven one day.

10

Choosing to Praise God

FROM THE MOUNTAINTOP

WE humans are a weird bunch. When we're in the pits, most of us are not of the mindset to praise God, and when we're on the mountaintop, we often fail to remember to thank God and to praise Him for His goodness. Truth is, we're far more likely to hit our knees when things are bad than when things are good. One would think it would be natural to praise God when everything is going well and when we're enjoying God's blessings and favor; however, it is then that we may forget who orchestrated our success; we might even take credit ourselves for something He brought about.

Knowing I'm quadriplegic, you can imagine I've faced plenty of adversity. But know that I've also had many mountaintop highs—those times when everything went right, when I felt loved and appreciated, when I experienced God's unmistakable hand of direction and affirmation on my life.

Much to my surprise, some of those highs have occurred in my life as a performer. In the late 1990s I began speaking at large women's conferences across the country. My first such opportunity was when I was invited to be a presenter at the Heritage Keepers Conference for five thousand women in Wichita, Kansas. Please understand that I am first and foremost a wife and mom, and my biggest credential as a speaker is my intimate relationship with Jesus. But when I was invited to present at this event, I felt inadequate because I didn't have a seminary or religious studies background, nor did I have a recording contract like the big Christian contemporary singers. So you will appreciate that I, excited and honored as I was to be invited, was at the same time totally intimidated to be sharing the stage with Kathy Troccoli and Point of Grace. To make matters worse, I heard that all the speakers were expected to be in the front row to support the other presenters at this conference. So these hugely popular and talented women of God, headliner recording artists whose talents I so admired, would be sitting right there in the front row hearing every word I said and every note I sang. I felt out of my league, even frightened.

With that knowledge looming heavily in my thoughts, I prepared very diligently to perfect every word and timed my presentation so that I would be on stage exactly thirty minutes, which was my allotted time.

And all my preparation and hard work, along with my family's prayers that my message would be well-received, paid off. I could feel the audience with me as I shared my testimony, and when I closed with singing "God Is in Control," all five thousand women were on their feet, singing with me with hands up, proclaiming confidently that God is indeed in control of our lives. Wow.

Because of my wheelchair, I couldn't just step off the stage and take my place in the front row, so during the applause, I rolled off stage and literally fell right into my husband's arms and started sobbing. I had done it. God had done it! I was overwhelmed to think that I had been effective in this setting.

When I collected myself a bit, we went down the backstage elevator and out into the hallway. I was trying to make my way back into the arena when I heard, "Renée? Where is Renée? Kathy is calling for her!" Suddenly, Mike and I were pulled back into the arena as Kathy Troccoli yelled into the microphone, "Where's Renée? Get back in here!" As I rolled up to the base of the stage, applause broke out again. Kathy came down off the stage and whispered to me, "You are incredible! Do you know my song, 'Go Light Your World'?"

I said, "Of course!" I had sung it at our youth group at church many times.

She said, "Sing it with me now."

Since I no longer had a microphone, Kathy leaned over and, with our heads together, we shared the mic. As certain as I initially was that I knew the words, the second verse wasn't as familiar, so when I'd need help I'd look at her saying with my eyes, "Help me out!" and she would whisper the next line in my ear. As we were singing I was struck by how amazing it was. *I am singing with Kathy Troccoli!* The room was electric. The people were on their feet. It was a moment I'll always remember.

Afterward, Kathy gave me a big hug and I rolled off to park in the front row with the other speakers, and the applause just kept going and going and going. I kept trying to throw my hands toward Kathy to indicate, "It's her turn," but she lingered so we could receive the applause together. Then the music started for her program; she took the stage and did her whole concert, and it was such a joy to sit with the other speakers and watch the pro perform, knowing that I had been fully accepted and affirmed.

Wow, God! Look what You did! Definitely a mountaintop.

A similar thing happened to me when I was scheduled to appear at the National Christian Booksellers Association Convention in Anaheim with Sandi Patty—in my eyes, the most phenomenal soprano in Christian music. She is the gauge by whom most classically trained sopranos in church music judge talent. To say that I was intimidated was an understatement; scared out of my wits would have been closer to the truth.

The invitation to the convention came in 2002 when my first book, *The Last Dance but Not the Last*

Song, was released. I was invited by my publisher Fleming H. Revell to give my testimony and sing during Sunday morning worship. I was pretty amazed that I was given such a key spot. A week prior to the convention, our office received the morning schedule including my sound check time, and there in bold letters glaring at me I saw: "9:15 a.m.: Renée Bondi; 9:30 a.m.: Sandi Patty." *Sandi Patty?! I'm going to be on the same program with the ultimate Christian soprano of all time?*

Comparing myself to Sandi, I felt like a homemade dress being modeled beside an Oscar de la Renta. I have a background in classical music, but this was Christian music, and to me Sandi Patty was the whole package. I love her voice and her stage presence and have a real appreciation for her vocal technique. If you had told me that I would one day share the stage with Sandi Patty, I would've said, "Yeah, right. When donkeys fly."

I spent the whole week obsessing about the upcoming event, thinking I would never be good enough vocally to share the stage with the one and only Sandi Patty. I'm sure part of my insecurity comes from being quadriplegic; I still think that if I weren't sitting down and didn't have all this hardware around me that I would be a more effective performer. A performer communicates with her body—singing one song standing and another sitting, using expressive hands, moving the microphone up and down. She makes an entrance when she walks on stage, and I often feel that I just roll out and sit there. My choreography consists of head movements, limited arm raising, moving from one side of the stage to the other, and maybe a turnabout in my wheelchair. I am told that my audiences stop noticing my physical limitations after I've been speaking and singing for a while—praise God!—but I still feel restricted on stage.

Now I was to appear with one of the biggest performers I could imagine. I knew I would not be able to sing the high notes as powerfully as she, and I knew that I had to sing a few high F's because the organizers had specifically requested "Be Still and Hear My Voice," a song I wrote for our son. So there was no getting around singing high notes in front of Sandi Patty and several hundred people in that worship service. *Yikes.*

A few days before the event, I let my insecurities get the best of me. My stress resulted in a very stiff neck, and the muscles on my right side cramped up so much I couldn't even sit up in the wheelchair because of the pain. So before my caregiver left that morning, I asked her to lay me down, and I spent the day in bed.

My mom heard what was going on, and the sweetest thing happened. My dad, who is a rancher and not a touchy-feely kind of guy or one to show much emotion, walked into my bedroom, pulled up a chair, and sat down next to my bed. "So what's this I hear about your letting some singer intimidate you? Don't you know how good you are? I hear it from everyone I know! People stop me all the time and tell me that they heard you somewhere and say how touched they were! Why are you letting this gal intimidate you so much?"

Dad's talk helped because he reminded me of the people out there who God has touched through my voice; after all, CBA would not have invited me to speak and sing at their chapel service if they didn't think I had something to offer. It just never ceases to amaze and overwhelm me that God would use me! The pep talk really helped; it's a treasured memory I hold dear of my dad who has since passed away.

Inevitably Sunday morning dawned. I arrived thirty minutes early to give myself plenty of time to find the right hall in the huge Anaheim Convention Center. As I finished my sound check, Sandi walked toward me on the stage. As I turned and saw her, I exclaimed, "Oh my goodness! It's really you, and I finally get to meet you! I have to tell you that I've been freaked out all week since I heard that you and I would be sharing the platform. I am more than a little intimidated."

She laughed and replied, "Oh, there's no need to feel that way. I'll tell you why when I have a minute. After my sound check, we'll talk."

Later in the Green Room, Sandi pulled up a chair and sat down next to me and said, "Can I tell you something? I know how you feel. I'm scared to death to go out on that stage this morning. This is my first public performance since my divorce, and I don't know how I'll be received. The people may not accept me, and I am very nervous. For all I know, they might want to throw tomatoes at me."

I didn't even know she was divorced, so I certainly

couldn't offer anything on that subject. But my heart went out to her, and before I knew it I heard myself say, "Oh, Sandi, not every person in the audience knows what you've gone through. I didn't know until you told me right now! Yes, there will be some people who are aware, and it is their choice to receive what you have to say in your music or to reject it; that's between them and God. But I do know that God is very faithful, and He will not let you crumble on that stage. I'll be praying you through it."

Here I had assumed that Sandi would be the epitome of confidence. How touching for her to share and for me to know that she, at that time, was feeling just as unsure as I. She was very warm, transparent and real.

The worship service began. I gave my testimony and sang "Be Still," and I was deeply touched by the congregation's warm response of a standing ovation. Sandi watched me on the TV monitor in the Green Room, and when I left the stage, she met me at the door. She took my face in her hands and demanded, "How do you do that? How do you float up to those high notes while sitting down and paralyzed? How do you do that? You sounded gorgeous! I'm so impressed!" *Wow. The queen of Christian high notes complimenting my voice!* Sandi's kind words certainly put a smile on my face.

Lee Strobel gave the message and then Sandi closed the service with a beautiful performance. By the time she finished and returned, there were more people in the Green Room because it was the end of the service, so we didn't get much time to talk. However, I gave her a tight hug, and I thought she was going to cry. I could really feel her sense of relief that nobody had booed or thrown tomatoes or, worse yet, walked out, which may have been her biggest fear. She was enthusiastically and warmly received, as she deserved to be.

Later that evening I had time to reflect on the events of the day. *Good and gracious God, You are so faithful. It seems when I least expect it, You show up and work all things out for my good and the good of others. I realize I freaked out because I didn't slow my thoughts down enough to remember that You are with me. I praise You for who You are and for Your attention to me. Thank You, Jesus.*

Once again I realized I could actually speak and sing effectively at this level. God had taken me—a wife, mom and educator—and used me to minister to a hurting world. We can never predict where and how God will use us, can we?

Sharing the stage with big names like Sandi Patty, Point of Grace, and Kathy Troccoli are some of the biggest performing mountaintop experiences I've enjoyed. However, the highest peak had nothing to do with being on stage. My ultimate peak started with a simple phone call.

The day before our son Daniel was starting first grade, the phone rang. When I answered, I heard the voice of my mother-in-law, Sandra Bondi. After the initial greetings, she said, "Well, sweetheart, you did it."

"Did what?" I asked.

"You got Daniel to first grade!" When she said that, a flood of memories rolled over me, and I immediately started to cry. I couldn't believe that she remembered a simple comment I had made years earlier when Daniel was a newborn. My in-laws had stayed at our house for a week, helping with Daniel, which enabled my parents to be at the hospital to care for my sister Michelle who was still fighting for her life from an ATV accident that left her permanently paralyzed and in a wheelchair as well. (I know. It's crazy that our family was hit with two spinal cord injuries six years apart. If you want to know that story, take a look at chapter 13 in *The Last Dance but Not the Last Song*.)

So my in-laws were with us the first week of Daniel's life, helping with nighttime feedings, family dinners etc. At one point during that week, I was feeding Daniel, and I looked up at Sandra and said, "If I can just get him to first grade, I'll be okay."

I said that because the infant/toddler years were the most frightening for me; I was thinking of safety. *What if he runs across the street into an oncoming car? What if he chokes? What if he falls and I can't pick him up?* The thought of raising an infant, a toddler, without the use of my hands and feet was very scary. This was the part of starting a family as a quadriplegic that frightened me most. My disability and feelings of inadequacy caused me to fear for his physical well-being. I knew that once Daniel got to first grade he would be more independent. My physical assistance would be less essential, and my verbal parenting skill would become more important.

This reality had weighed heavily on my heart during those early years, but I'd forgotten that I'd ever made that comment. Only my thoughtful mother-in-law would remember what I had said six years earlier—let alone time it to call me the day before our son entered first grade! So I started crying with her on the phone, thanking her for remembering this major crossroad in our lives.

The next day at 7:45 a.m. my caregiver dropped Daniel and me off at his school. Daniel jumped on the back of my wheelchair as he often did at that age, and we wheeled into the recreational area where the students gathered for morning assembly.

When I rolled onto that playground, a flood of emotions washed over me. I quietly said, "Okay, Daniel, jump off. I love you and am proud of you. Have a great first day!" I gave him a quick kiss, and he ran and got in line. I saw many mothers and fathers with their cameras and was aware of all that first day excitement, but I had to quietly, quickly roll around behind the gym to be alone. There, I proceeded to break down and weep.

My mother-in-law was right; I had made it. God was faithful! Daniel was healthy and normal and darling. My husband was amazing, kind and gentle and still willing to put up with me in my wheelchair. My sister was healthy and had adapted to her new life in her wheelchair. She had made it. I had made it. I knew

I had many years with Daniel ahead of me—lest I forget the teenage years!—but the scariest part for me was over, and I had made it!

That day was one of the highest mountaintop achievements I have ever experienced. Daniel was my very special gift from God, and as I sat there behind the gym, I remembered how Mike and I had prayed about our decision to bring a child into the family; we had decided to give God the opportunity to give us a child and leave the choice to Him. One month later I was pregnant. Very few women with my disability have children; either they can't or they choose not to. Is it any surprise that I was emotional over this milestone?

Sitting there, I thought of getting Daniel to doctors' appointments, arranging play dates, hiring an attendant so that an able-bodied person would be present in case of an emergency, etc. Although finances were a huge concern, I never stayed alone with Daniel in the house during those early years. And now he was six and totally normal, healthy, well-adjusted and delightful. Having a quad for a mom did not hinder or scar him at all.

As I sat there alone behind the gym, I looked up to the heavens and praised God for my son, and I thanked Him for His faithfulness and for helping me get him safely to first grade. And now, to bring you up to today, Daniel is a senior in high school. He's healthy, happy and confident, and may I add that he's also a really nice guy, just like his dad.

It would seem logical that we would automatically praise God in these high moments, but unfortunately, that's not true. Chapter 8 of Deuteronomy gives us explicit instructions for such times. On the banks of the River Jordan just before the Israelites were to move in and take the Promised Land, Moses had a talk with the people. He reminded them of where they had been: God had miraculously brought them out of slavery in Egypt, but then because of their unbelief, God had caused them to wander aimlessly in the wilderness for forty years. After this brief history reminder, Moses gave instructions for the future. He told them that because of what God had done, it was (and is) clear that He is worthy to be followed, honored and trusted. Because of what He expects, they should listen and obey. Because of who He is, they should love Him completely. Learning these lessons would prepare them to possess the Promised Land. These words are just as applicable to us today.

The Israelites had witnessed and experienced God's power and love, and soon they would see even more miracles like the parting of the Jordan or the conquest of Jericho when the walls collapsed when they, following God's instructions, marched around in silence seven times and then erupted in shouts. We remember God while in the battle, but we must also remember Him when the battle is won. That's why Moses admonished the Israelites, "Beware that you do not forget the LORD your God by not keeping His commandments and His ordinances and His statutes" (8:11, NASB).

Getting Daniel to first grade was my greatest "Promised Land" thus far. And with that, having a husband who loves me in spite of my wheelchair, having an extended family who love and support me and each other, seeing Michelle adjusting to her wheelchair, and having a few wow moments as a performer—all Promised Land successes.

What has been your "Promised Land"? Maybe the birth of your children, a promotion at work, an award, a victory, recovering from an illness, reconciliation with someone who was estranged. Like the Israelites, you and I have triumphs to remember. When we're not on the mountaintop; we can think back and see God's faithfulness and thank Him for it, and that gives us hope and trust for tomorrow.

When you're entering your Promised Land, *do not forget*. When life is rough and the road is uphill, *do not forget*. Or when you're just rocking along and life is uneventful, do not forget. And when you're on the mountaintop, *do not forget the Lord your God*.

Let's Talk It Over

I WISH I were sitting beside you right now. I'd love to know what you're thinking after reading the stories in this book, reviewing the Scriptures, analyzing the whole concept of praising and thanking God even when your journey is uphill. I'd love to talk to you and hear your thoughts, so let's imagine that we're in a little café enjoying a cup of coffee or tea together, and let's talk about this whole worship idea.

Now that you've become aware of the subject, you'll notice that Scripture is full of verses about praise. It's interesting that most of these verses were voiced by people who were facing enormous obstacles, great loss, injustice and a multitude of other difficult situations. David, Jehoshaphat, Leah, Gideon, Naomi, Mary, Paul and Silas all had uphill climbs, but all chose to trust and praise God, and they found Him to be faithful. They set examples for us to follow.

Jehoshaphat had a huge army coming at him. What battle are you facing right now? What forces are coming at you? Perhaps you are in a marriage gone sour, maybe you have a teenager who is making poor choices, possibly you or someone you love is fighting cancer or another devastating disease. In these times remember and take heart that the prophet told Jehoshaphat and his people that the Lord was saying, "Do not be afraid or discouraged because of this vast army. For the battle is not yours, but God's" (2 Chron. 20:15). That's for you and me as well; the battle is not ours, but the Lord's if we ask Him to be in control.

Not surprisingly, this prophecy was pronounced immediately after Jehoshaphat had assembled the people to praise God. So do you believe that Jehoshaphat leading the people in praise had something to do with God's presence? I think that's exactly the point. Throughout Scripture when the people worship God, He shows up!

I think we can safely assume that God put all those stories and characters in the Bible for a reason, and that reason is that He wants to teach us through their examples. King David thought it important to praise the Lord while facing huge projects and battles. Remember in First Chronicles 23 when David was preparing his son Solomon to build the temple to honor the Lord, he designated four thousand men to be gatekeepers and then four thousand to praise the Lord with musical instruments while the Temple was being built. It blows me away that David ordained the same number of worship musicians as security guards! I'd say David thought that spiritual protection was as important as physical protection!

And what of all the others? Paul thought it important to praise God even when imprisoned and in chains, and King Jehoshaphat and Mary and even Jesus Himself all praised God. If it was important for them, it must be important for us! Right?

So why isn't praise and worship always a natural outpouring of our love and adoration for our Lord? As I've mentioned, praising and thanking God during the tough times doesn't always come naturally. At least it didn't for me. I had to learn it, and I am still reminding myself to put it into practice when things are painful or stressful. I'm a little embarrassed to say that you won't find a lot of praise songs on my first two CDs. Rather, you'll find music of comfort because, in the first few years after my injury, I went to the Lord for strength, comfort and direction. It was hard for me to raise my hands and sing, "Hallelujah! Praise the Lord!" because I was ever so aware of my wheelchair. Those first weeks, months and years were a learning time; I was trying to cope with a situation that I never imagined would be mine.

Now I've learned to apply the "sacrifice of praise" that Hebrews 13:15 talks about. A sacrifice of praise is an offering of praise to God. When I first read it, I thought that the word "sacrifice" only suggested hardship—like "grit your teeth and do it whether you want to or not!" But that's not the only meaning at all. Because Jesus became the "Lamb of God" who was sacrificed in our place, animal sacrifices are now obsolete. So instead of offering God our animal sacrifice, we now offer our praise sacrifice. Beautiful, isn't it?

When looking deeper into the concept of praising God when we don't feel like it, I ran across another Scripture that stopped me in my tracks. "For although they knew God, they neither glorified him as God nor gave thanks to him. Although they claimed to be wise, they became fools and exchanged the glory of the immortal God for images made to look like mortal man and birds and animals and reptiles" (Rom. 1:21–23). We are created to praise God (Isa. 43:21). If we stop praising Him, our hearts are hardened and we start praising something else.

When Jesus was in the wilderness, Satan promised to give Jesus all the kingdoms of the world and their glory if Jesus would worship him, but Jesus replied, "Worship the Lord your God, and serve him only" (Matt. 4:10). Sometimes getting our focus off the Holy One and onto something we can have right now may be deceptively attractive, but we, like Jesus, must keep our eyes on the One who will never fail us.

So if you're not praising God, who or what are you worshiping? If you don't know the answer, then ask yourself, "What or who consumes my time, my energy, my thoughts and my money? Who or what takes more of my attention, adoration and interest than God?"

Let's consider what your answer could be. Is it your spouse (or finding one!)? Your children, darlings that they are? Your career, and along with it power, prestige, financial security? Sports heroes and/or celebrities? Your own intellect, abilities and success? Your popularity? I hate to tell you, but if anything—anything at all—is taking priority over your relationship with God, it's an idol whether you want to call it that or not.

Did any of the things mentioned in the last paragraph resonate for you? Have you stopped praising the Lord and begun praising something else? If so, allow me to gently take your shoulders and turn you back toward the Father, to put my fingers on your chin and tilt your head up. Let's stop focusing our attention on what the world offers and start praising God!

Perhaps at one time you had a heart full of praise for your Lord, but somewhere along the way life happened, and you got sidetracked or derailed. It's kind of like a recipe that you used to prepare often because you loved it, then one day you realize you haven't prepared that dish in a long time, and you wonder why you stopped. Somehow it just slipped off the list. Scripture acknowledges that tendency in our spiritual walk: "You have forsaken your first love. Remember the height from which you have fallen! Repent and do the things you did at first" (Rev 2:4–5). God does not take our lack of devotion lightly. The first phrase of that verse is, "Yet I hold this against you." I don't know about you, but I certainly don't want anything to be in my life that God would hold against me.

So what does praising the Lord do? Worship always brings you into God's presence and into alignment with His throne. Isaiah 6:1 says, "I saw the Lord seated on a throne, high and exalted, and the train of his robe filled the temple." What a vision! Imagine seeing that! Being Christian for many years now, I've become a bit more keen on recognizing the Lord's presence in my life. The way it's come about is from one thing—worshiping Him. In other words, we are more likely to see the King high and exalted and to be reminded of His faithfulness when we sit at His feet.

When we sit at the King's feet, we are creating what I like to call habits of faith. When we are diligent in going to God and praising Him when life is relatively calm, then we will continue to do so when the sea of life gets stormy. As Oswald Chambers pointed out in *My Utmost for His Highest*, "When a crisis arises, we instantly reveal upon whom we rely. If we have been learning to worship God and to place our trust in Him, the crisis will reveal that we can go to the point of breaking, yet without breaking our confidence in Him."[1] And that confidence is what gives us peace amidst the storm.

---

1. Chambers, Oswald and Reimann, James, ed., *My Utmost for His Highest*, Discovery House Publishers: Grand Rapids, MI, 1992. August 12 entry

In addition, we can't really know the depth of our character until we see how we react under a trial. "Blessed is the man who perseveres under trial, because when he has stood the test, he will receive the crown of life that God has promised to those who love him" (James 1:12). Sister and brother, I see the jewels sparkling in your crown right now. Hang in there! Keep going!

Thanking and praising the Lord changes my heart. "Those who live according to the flesh have their minds set on what the flesh desires; but those who live in accordance with the Spirit have their minds set on what the Spirit desires. The mind governed by the flesh is death, but the mind governed by the Spirit is life and peace" (Rom. 8:5–6). It's up to us to set our minds on what the Spirit desires. That is how we make choices in the daylight that will sustain us in the darkness. It's a bit like physical fitness or a diet; it takes discipline and deliberate right choices.

The more I spend time at the feet of Jesus, the more I trust Him. It's like a good friendship or marriage to me—the more you spend good, quality time with your friend laughing, sharing your heart and your concerns, the more you can trust that person to always look out for your best interests. I think it's very much the same way with God. It's hard to trust Him when you haven't gotten to know His character. There's that lyric again—"If you can't see God's hand, trust His heart." We know by His character that He will never forsake us, but we can't know His character if we don't spend time with Him.

In John 4:23 Jesus is speaking to the woman at the well and explaining to her that worship is not defined by a particular place or form: "Yet a time is coming and has now come when the true worshipers will worship the Father in spirit and truth, for they are the kind of worshipers the Father seeks." The Father seeks worshipers! Is God some kind of arrogant egomaniac who needs to be praised and adored? No, God does not *need* our praise. It is we who have the need! We need to praise God so that we keep our focus on Him—our Savior, the Creator, the Great Comforter and Healer.

And so, dear reader, my desire for you is that no matter where you are on your spiritual journey—if you're just beginning, if you've been walking with Jesus for many years or if you're somewhere in between—that *Still, I Will Praise* has opened your mind and heart to the value of choosing to praise God in all circumstances.

As our time together here comes to a close, know that I have prayed for you. And now I invite you to open your heart and pray with me:

I will praise you, O Lord my God, with all my heart;
I will glorify your name forever.
For great is your love toward me;
you have delivered me from the depths of the grave.
Psalm 86:12–13

Now to the King eternal, immortal, invisible, the only God,
be honor and glory for ever and ever. Amen.
Timothy 1:17

A Call to Action

STUDY GUIDE FOR DEEPER REFLECTION

THIS guide is intended to help you dig deeper into your relationship with our Lord by experiencing the value of praising Him through painful times. The action points require time and focus. Please read them prayerfully and with a Bible on hand. (If you are new to reading Scripture, the table of contents is your best friend!) I know God wants to speak to you, and I pray you will sense more of Him as you choose to praise Him in all things.

For Starters

Maybe you're reading this book but have never experienced the full joy of Christ living in you. Let me assure you that He loves you and wants to guide you into the peace and security that come from knowing Him. Will you pray with me? *Dear Jesus, I want to know You more intimately than I do now. I know that I am broken and that I have sinned, and I ask You to forgive and restore me. I thank You for dying on the cross for me so that I might have new, abundant, real life in You. Please help me trust You more, and open my eyes to recognize the ways in which You're moving in my life. You are my Lord, and I thank You. Amen.*

Chapter 1: *Choosing to Praise God* **in Times of Frustration**

 First Peter 5:6–11. Because of God's loving care for us, we're able to rest in who He is. God is not only *able* to carry our burdens, He *wants* to free you from your anxieties so we can live in peace. What currently is causing you stress? Write down a few of these "stressors" in your life, and surrender each one individually to God, visualizing yourself laying your burden at Jesus' feet.

_____

_____

_____

_____

 Being centered in the Lord gives us hope for a brighter tomorrow. When we're struggling with something, we have the blessed assurance that if we rely on God, He will renew us inside and prepare us for a greater glory. Read Second Corinthians 4:16–17. Write a prayer to the Lord thanking Him for His daily presence and provision.

_____

_____

_____

_____

_____

ଔ Make a list of several reasons you have to praise God right now. Whenever you start feeling overwhelmed, return to the list and add more.

_____

_____

_____

_____

_____

_____

Chapter 2: *Choosing to Praise God* **in Times of Unanswered Prayer**

ଔ Read Psalm 37:7. What prayer are you still waiting to see God answer? Although waiting on the Lord can be difficult, it's important to trust Him to work out every situation for your best (even if it isn't what you have imagined as being "best"). Write down what you're asking the Lord to do, and then keep track of how He moves in the situation. (Remember—it might not be what you expect!)

_____

_____

_____

_____

❧ Scripture reveals that God has a heart for those who are pained and marginalized. Don't allow yourself to believe the lie that God doesn't hear you when you cry to Him. Spend some time meditating on Psalm 34:17–18.

❧ Read Proverbs 6:6–8 and Matthew 6:25–34. Take some time to consider the smallest of God's creation. Record what you see. Ask God to show you more of who He is through the things He has made.

_____

_____

_____

_____

_____

Chapter 3: Choosing to Praise God When You Need a Second Chance

Know that even when it feels like your world is falling apart, God is working to redeem your situation. Seeing something as a catastrophe or as a blessing depends on your perspective. Imagine that you're out to sea on a boat in a storm. The wind is raging and waves are crashing all around you. Cold water is washing across the deck, and you're struggling to stay on board. The sky is dark and ominous; there's no end in sight to the storm. Now imagine that you're watching the same storm from a lighthouse, safe on the shore. The storm is no less violent, but you no longer fear for your life. You might even recognize beauty in the lightning and whitecaps. You see, God doesn't always remove us from situations, but He does give us a new perspective on them. When we're secure in Him, we can weather any storm. Write about a time when you felt the Lord's presence through one of life's storms. (If nothing comes to mind, ask someone who you know is strong in the Lord to give you an example from his/her life.) _____

_____

_____

_____

_____

_____

_____

ငွ God gives us many promises in Scripture, and we can stand firm on them. Memorize Isaiah 54:10.

ငွ Read John 8:1–11. Identify something in your past that has caused you shame and, as a result, is holding you back. Write it down on a slip of paper, confess it to God and ask His forgiveness, thank Him for forgiving you, and then tear the paper into as many pieces as possible. Know that when you ask for forgiveness, God is quick to remove your sins "as far as the east is from the west" (Ps. 103:12). Rest in His grace and compassion.

ငွ God wants to know you intimately. Knowing Him is loving Him, and loving Him is trusting Him. Write a love letter to the Lord.

_____

_____

_____

_____

_____

_____

Chapter 4: *Choosing to Praise God **in Times of Waiting***

ଛ Read Philippians 4:8. What is true or right or lovely in your life right now? The sun coming up? Having a shirt on your back? A flower blooming in the yard?

Below you will find the eight adjectives that Paul invites us to consider. To the right of each adjective, write something in your life that fits that description:

True _____

Noble _____

Right _____

Pure _____

Lovely _____

Admirable _____

Excellent _____

Praiseworthy _____

ଛ Read Philippians 1:6. Isn't it great that when God starts something, He always sees it through to its finish? List some things that God has called you to do—for example, parenting, teaching children at church, fulfilling your responsibilities in the workplace, volunteering to help the needy. Whatever God has given you to do, rest in the assurance that He who began the good work in you will be faithful to complete it.

_____

_____

_____

_____

ଔ What's one of your favorite hymns or praise songs? Write a verse here that particularly resonates with you and why.

_____

_____

_____

_____

_____

Chapter 5: Choosing to Praise God **When Things Go from Bad to Worse**

ଔ Read David's lament in Psalm 119:107–108.
It's okay to admit that you're struggling with a hard situation, but if you can direct your attention to God and His goodness, then you can recognize that God can work through even the darkest circumstances.

Write your own psalm to the Lord or rewrite the verse above in your own words. (Remember that while

David was often upset about his environment, he maintained proper perspective by praising the Lord and reaffirming his trust in God's plan.)

_____

_____

_____

_____

_____

_____

_____

ଓ Read Colossians 3:17. Write a few actions or activities you must do this week that you don't particularly enjoy. Later, as you begin each task, choose to pray saying, *I do this in Your name, my Lord Jesus Christ, and I thank You for being with me and providing the necessary grace to do this task well and without complaining!*

_____

_____

_____

_____

ଓ Read Psalm 46:1–3:

As a shepherd, David likely had to literally weather some pretty serious storms while tending his flock. He wrote about what he knew—that even when things looked dark, God was there.

Think about one of the scariest, most threatening things you've had to face. Maybe it's being in an accident or a storm or financial crisis. Now write a few lines about that time, but instead of writing despairingly, write like David. Start with the line, "God is our refuge and strength, an ever-present help in trouble," and go from there.

_____

_____

_____

_____

_____

_____

Chapter 6: *Choosing to Praise God* **in Times of Loneliness**

୦୫ One of the best ways to fight a feeling of loneliness is to focus on something outside of yourself. Write down a few random acts of kindness you could do for a particular person. They don't have to be big, but they should be from the heart. (Ex. 1: Send a note of encouragement to your child's teacher. Ex. 2: Call someone who needs help with transportation and volunteer to take him/her to run errands.)

_____

_____

_____

_____

_____

_____

_____

ଓ When you're feeling like you don't fit in, remember that God made every person to be unique, and He has a specific purpose for you. When we use the gifts and talents God has given us in community and in service to others, it gives us a sense of fulfillment and of purpose. Read First Corinthians 12, and spend some time praying and asking God to show you how He has gifted you.

Do you like spending time with kids? Do you enjoy encouraging others? Do you know how to make great cookies? Each of these can be used in practical ways to show God's love. Think back over your past month and write down a few moments you enjoyed (everything from successfully fixing a flat on your car to being kind to the cashier at the grocery store) and then look for more ways to keep serving others (another type of sacrifice of praise)!

_____

_____

_____

_____

_____

_____

_____

_____

ଓ In our most devastating times of suffering, it's very difficult to see God's hand in our lives. In Matthew 28:20 Jesus promises, "I am with you always, to the very end of the age." List five different names used for Jesus in Scripture. Quietly read this list aloud several times focusing on who He is.

_____

_____

_____

_____

_____

Chapter 7: *Choosing to Praise God* **in Times of Great Loss**

ଔ Read Psalm 147:3. If you're feeling broken, do you believe God will heal you? Will you accept the peace He can give you, or does some part of you still feel hopelessly angry? Write an honest prayer, telling God how you feel, and ask Him to change your heart to welcome His healing.

_____

_____

_____

_____

_____

ଔ Read Colossians 3:15–16. Identify three things today for which you are thankful. Take ten minutes to quietly praise God for those three things. Yes, take the entire ten minutes!

_____

_____

_____

_____

❧ It's often most difficult to see God's hand in our lives in our greatest times of suffering, but like any good parent, He wants us to come to Him with both our joy and our deep grief. And better than any earthly parent, He can bear our burdens so we, like Jana, can worship through the darkest days. Spend some time meditating on Matthew 11:28–30.

Chapter 8: *Choosing to Praise God **When You're Afraid***

❧ Read Joshua 1:9. What does the Lord tell us to do in this verse? What does He say not to do? What is the key piece that allows us to follow these commands?

_____

_____

_____

_____

_____

❧ Read Second Timothy 1:7. When you're feeling fearful or uncertain, remember that God has graced you with His power to conquer your problem, His love to comfort you through your trial, and the self-discipline needed to trust Him when the road gets rough. Notice that facing your struggle with an attitude of victory (rather than insecurity) gives you a posture of strength–strength in the Lord. What are a few practical ways you can live out the truth of this verse? (Ex: When you run into someone who rubs you the wrong way, you can thank God for giving you the power to choose to love that person. Ask Him to help you see from His perspective.)

_____

_____

_____

_____

_____

_____

ଔ Think of a fear you might have that is robbing you of full joy. Declare out loud that, through the power of the blood Jesus shed to save you, you rebuke the powers of evil that are trapping you in anxiety and uncertainty, which are not of God.

*Chapter 9: Choosing to Praise God **When Things Look Hopeless***

ଔ There is a specific time for everything in God's plan. Read Psalm 30, and notice how joy follows a time of sorrow. What does this Psalm reveal about God's character? How does it make you feel that a day of rejoicing is coming? How do you plan to celebrate when God turns your weeping into rejoicing?

_____

_____

_____

_____

_____

_____

_____

ଔ Read Isaiah 40:28–31.

What does this verse reveal about God's character? Write how believing that God is who this verse says He is allows you to face life with a renewed perspective. (Ex: Because I know God is everlasting, I have hope in a bright future in heaven with Him!)

_____

_____

_____

_____

_____

_____

ଔ Read Exodus 15:11. Identify several of the wonders in this world that you know no one could have made but God—the sun, a hummingbird, the optical nerve allowing you to see this page, etc.

_____

_____

_____

_____

_____

_____

Chapter 10: *Choosing to Praise God **from the Mountaintop***

ଔ Identify your mountaintop experiences of the past year, and list a few here. (If you are in a tough place and feel that there weren't any, remember the simple things—the fact that you can read this page, the fact that you have a bed to sleep in.) Begin a daily habit of praising Him for all things, small and large.

_____

_____

_____

_____

_____

_____

_____

ଜ Take a praise song, memorize it and then sing or speak it throughout the week to help keep your eyes on the Lord.

ଜ Read slowly John 4:1–26. Besides the obvious, what do you learn about who Jesus is? What do you learn about having the Holy Spirit in your heart when you worship?

_____

_____

_____

_____

_____

_____

_____

_____

_____

The LORD is my rock, my fortress and my deliverer;
   my God is my rock, in whom I take refuge.
   He is my shield and the horn of my salvation, my stronghold.
I call to the LORD, who is worthy of praise,
   and I am saved from my enemies.

Psalm 18:2–3

Also by Renée

The Last Dance But Not The Last Song
by Renée Bondi with Nancy Curtis.
Renée's story will take you on one
of the most incredible life journeys
you can imagine, and one that is sure
to leave a lasting impression. Read the
complete story and witness God's providence.

*This 285 page book includes color photo
insert.*

Mercies in Disguise
Renée's angelic voice spotlights God's loving
kindness and intimate mercy that often seem
disguised when viewed by a hurting heart.

Twelve songs including: "Be Not Afraid,"
"On Eagle's Wings," "Blessings," "Amazing
Grace" and "When God Ran."

All recordings are available on **CD** or **downloads.**

order online at **www.reneebondi.com**

or call **1-800-795-5757**

Let It Rain

This personal signature collection of original songs finds Renée reflecting on the power of God's grace raining down on our lives.

Ten songs including: "The Last Dance but Not the Last Song," "I Can Do All Things (Phil 4:13)," "Be Still" and "We Will Rise Again."

Surrender to Your Love

Renée invites us to jump with full abandon into the abundant life God has planned for each of us.

Twelve songs including: "Surrender," "Shout to the Lord," "Thank You," "God Is in Control," "You Are Mine" and "Holy is Your Name."

Strength for the Journey

This recording inspires listeners to move past their pain and seek Christ's peace.

Twelve songs including: "Firm Foundation," "Strength for the Journey," "Dream High," "He Who Began a Good Work in You," "Only in God" and "Somebody's Prayin'."

My Christmas Wish

For years fans have asked to hear Renée's voice singing their favorite Christmas Carols. Who better to sing songs of hope and joy!

Twelve songs including: "What Child Is This," "Silent Night," "Ave Maria," "O Holy Night," "Hark! the Herald Angels Sing" and "Sleigh Ride."

This book was produced by CLC Publications. We hope it has been life-changing and has given you a fresh experience of God through the work of the Holy Spirit. CLC Publications is an outreach of CLC Ministries International, a global literature mission with work in over fifty countries. If you would like to know more about us or are interested in opportunities to serve with a faith mission, we invite you to contact us at:

CLC Ministries International
PO Box 1449
Fort Washington, PA 19034

Phone: 215-542-1242
E-mail: orders@clcpublications.com
Website: www.clcpublications.com

DO YOU LOVE GOOD CHRISTIAN BOOKS?
Do you have a heart for worldwide missions?

You can receive a FREE subscription to
CLC's newsletter on global literature missions
Order by e-mail at:

clcworld@clcusa.org

Or fill in the coupon below and mail to:

PO Box 1449
Fort Washington, PA 19034

FREE *CLC WORLD* SUBSCRIPTION!

Name: _____

Address:_____

_____

Phone: _____ **E-mail:**_____

READ THE REMARKABLE STORY OF
the founding of
CLC International

Leap of Faith

"Any who doubt that Elijah's God still lives ought to read of the money supplied when needed, the stores and houses provided, and the appearance of personnel in answer to prayer." —Moody Monthly

Is it possible that the printing press, the editor's desk, the Christian bookstore and the mail order department can glow with the fast-moving drama of an "Acts of the Apostles"?

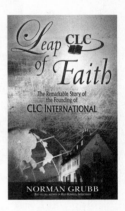

Find the answer as you are carried from two people in an upstairs bookroom to a worldwide chain of Christian bookcenters multiplied by nothing but a "shoestring" of faith and by committed, though unlikely, lives.

The

CLC BIBLE COMPANION

"I commend this book with enthusiasm . . . It contains accurate information, which is presented in a balanced and readable form. [The essential truths of Christianity and Christian living will] . . .
. . . "stimulate Bible readers to a deeper study of the great Christian fundamentals, . . . assist busy preachers plan their teachings, . . . and be a great benefit for group studies."

-Rev. John Stott, rector emeritus, All Souls Church

(hard cover) ISBN: 978-1-936143-13-9
(flexible cover) ISBN: 978-1-936143-23-8
(electronic version) ISBN: 978-1-936143-24-5

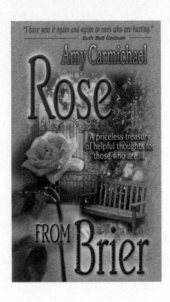

ROSE FROM BRIER

Amy Carmichael

"Miss Carmichael was inspired to write this book by reflecting that most books of comfort for sick people are written by the well, and so miss their mark.

Thus, from her own personal experiences, she has gathered a priceless treasury of helpful thoughts for those who are ill. This is why it "speaks to our condition" and why I have sent it again and again to ones who are hurting. As pain is not always physical, **it is a book for all who suffer. It is by far the best that I have found.**" *Ruth Bell Graham*

ISBN: 978-0-87508-077-2

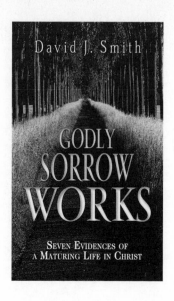

GODLY SORROW WORKS

David J. Smith

"*If you have a hunger in your heart to know God more intimately and to experience His grace more fully, you will find the wisdom here to be practical, penetrating and perceptive. It was good for me to read it, and it will be good for you too.*" Dennis Kinlaw, Chancellor, Asbury College

ISBN: 978-0-87508-775-7

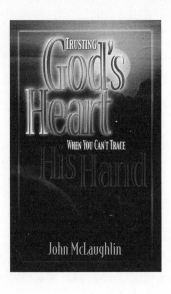

TRUSTING GOD'S HEART
WHEN YOU CAN'T TRACE HIS HAND

John McLaughlin

Through the ancient biblical account of Abraham's sacrifice of Isaac, God prophetically enacts the story of the cross: for it's in the cross that the question of God's love is forever settled.

This book helps readers understand God's immeasureable love for them through the experiences of Abraham and Jesus. If in this life you strive to be a victor and not a victim, then you must begin "TRUSTING GOD'S HEART WHEN YOU CAN'T TRACE HIS HAND."

ISBN: 978-0-87508-592-0

TOO SOON TO QUIT!

Warren W. Wiersbe

Ready to quit? You're not the only one. Flip through the pages of Scripture—you're in good company. Warren Wiersbe unfolds the stories of fifteen Bible characters who struggled just like you, and tells how you can gain the strength to survive—and thrive—when the road gets rocky.

ISBN: 978-1-936143-00-9

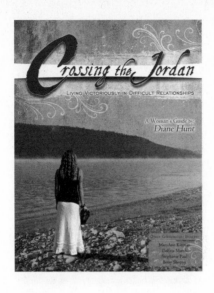

CROSSING THE JORDAN!

America's Keswick / Diane Hunt;
contributions from America's Keswick's
women's ministry staff

Are you ready to leave the wilderness of bitterness to live in Christ's promised land of freedom and peace? *Crossing the Jordan* will teach you how to respond to your loved one caught in addiction—but are you ready to get your feet wet?

ISBN: 978-1-936143-22-1

YOU WANT ME TO DO WHAT?

Elizabeth L. Smoot

Do you ever wonder what you've gotten yourself into now that you've decided to be a stay-at-home mom? Do you feel strong and bold some days, yet inadequate on other days? If you're shaking your head yes, you are not alone.

Elizabeth writes this devotional to encourage mothers as they stay at home and mold children for eternity.

So don't say, "You want me to do WHAT for the next few years?" Instead say, "God, I can't wait to see what You and I are going to do with this little family of mine!"

ISBN: 978-0-87508-202-8

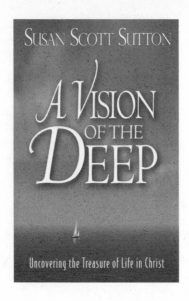

A VISION OF THE DEEP

Susan Scott Sutton

Susan Sutton takes us beyond a sense of obligation and responsibility in the Christian life to give us a "vision of the deep." If you are dissatisfied with "surface living," join Susan in this life-altering venture to lose yourself in the fathomless depths of Jesus Christ.

ISBN: 978-0-87508-786-3

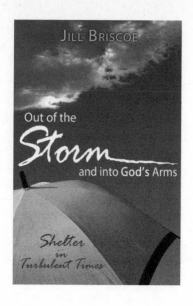

OUT OF THE STORM
AND INTO GOD'S ARMS

Jill Briscoe

What do you do when the storm clouds of life surround you—and you can't see the silver lining? Where do you turn when God feels distant? Exploring truths from the book of Job, Jill Briscoe addresses the tough issues involved in the collision of affliction and faith.

ISBN: 978-1-61958-008-4